GODMODE

Unlocking Your Creative Superpowers

Phillip Mitchell Polite

PAGE PUBLISHING
Conneaut Lake, PA

First originally published by Page Publishing 2024

ISBN 979-8-89157-439-7 (pbk)
ISBN 979-8-89157-451-9 (digital)

Printed in the United States of America

1

The Gift of Vision

In the ancient pages of the Bible, one figure stands out as a true visionary—Abraham. His story is one of profound inspiration, illustrating the incredible power of vision that transcends the boundaries of time and space.

Abraham's journey begins in the land of Ur, where he lived with his family. Despite the comfort and familiarity of his surroundings, Abraham had a vision that extended far beyond the horizon of his everyday life. He saw more than just the immediate reality; he saw a future that shimmered with possibilities, like a distant star beckoning him forward. What set Abraham apart was not merely the ability to dream or imagine but the unwavering belief in the reality of his vision. He didn't just have a vague notion of a brighter future; he possessed a profound inner knowing that what he saw was destined to become a reality. This vision was no small feat. It called upon him to leave behind the safety and security of his homeland, to venture into the unknown, and to embrace a path filled with challenges and uncertainties. But Abraham's unshakable faith in his vision was the driving force behind his courage. It propelled him to take that remarkable journey, guided by a higher purpose and a divine calling. In many ways, Abraham's story serves as a timeless testament to the transformative power of vision. It reminds us that vision isn't confined to the realm of dreams; it's a force that can shape the course of our lives. It's the ability to see beyond obstacles, to envision a brighter future, and to summon the determination to turn that vision into a reality.

As we delve into the essence of vision in *GodMode*, we'll draw inspiration from Abraham's unwavering belief and determination. We'll explore how the gift of vision, like that distant star, can guide us through the uncharted territory of creativity, urging us to embark on our unique and remarkable journeys. We often find ourselves seeking inspiration beyond the mundane, glimpsing the heavens for moments of heightened creativity and boundless genius.

We look to the stars, to gods and goddesses for the spark that ignites our creative fires. Yet amidst this quest for transcendence, we often forget a profound truth: the Divine dwells within us, and in our most inspired moments, we touch the heavens.

As I stand here at the crossroads of my own journey, I've traversed the deserts of despair and delved into the limitless. Through these adventures, I've come to a realization: we are not mere mortals seeking the divine; we are immortal souls graced with the power to touch the heavens in moments of heightened creativity.

It was in 2003, amid the chaos of Iraq, that I began to understand the depths of human spirit and the significance of sacrifice. But it was in the years that followed, in the mesmerizing world of entertainment and creative arts, that I discovered a state of existence I've come to call "GodMode."

"GodMode" is a zone. A divine state of consciousness where creativity flows effortlessly, where the lines between inspiration and creation blur, and where we reach out to touch the heavens. It's an experience we all possess the potential to unlock, a reminder of our immortal souls awaiting recognition.

In the pages ahead, we will embark on a journey through the annals of time and the recesses of our own consciousness. We will draw inspiration from the depths of history, the wisdom of diverse cultures, and the immortal souls of creative giants who have soared beyond ordinary limits. Together, we will explore the superpowers latent within us, waiting to be awakened. Each chapter will introduce a God superpower—a gift or talent encoded in our very essence—and illuminate it with a historical example. We will delve into the lives of visionaries, creators, and luminaries who, in their moments of divine inspiration, touched the heavens with their work. Through their stories and our own, we will uncover the keys to ascending to higher levels of consciousness, where our immortal souls find resonance.

This journey is not about becoming gods but recognizing that the Divine resides within us all. It's a call to embrace meditation, self-discovery, and the transcendent potential of creativity. It's an invitation to journey through GodMode and, in doing so, to reconnect with our immortal souls.

So, fellow explorers of the cosmos, let us commence this odyssey into the heart of creativity and consciousness. Armed with the knowledge that we are more than mere mortals, that our souls are immortal, let us embrace the divine within and reach out to touch the heavens in moments of extraordinary inspiration.

Welcome to GodMode, where the infinite awaits within.

*****

Creativity and moments of divine clarity are like sudden bursts of light in the darkest of nights, illuminating the path ahead with an uncanny and undeniable truth. For me, these moments have been nothing short of revelations, a testament to the gift of vision that resides within us all.

I recall a night in the heart of Northern Iraq, attached to the 173rd Airborne Division amidst the relentless chaos of a combat zone, when I felt the presence of something inexplicable. It was as if the universe itself had whispered in my ear, revealing a somber truth before its time. A vision of impending loss, a premonition that chilled me to the bone. I couldn't ignore it, and tragically, it unfolded as foretold.

But life is a tapestry woven with threads of both shadow and light. In the same desolate place, where the weight of the world pressed upon my shoulders, I discovered that the gift of vision isn't confined to foreseeing tragedy. It's a portal to boundless creativity, even in the face of adversity.

I found myself there, under great pressure, with creativity as my only refuge. Amidst the dust and uncertainty, I was crafting a novel—a tale that flowed from me like water from a mountain spring. It was a vivid assortment of characters, emotions, and worlds, unfolding before my eyes with an energy I could only describe as divine. Even under the harshest circumstances, creativity surged and art flourished. I never released or even finished the book, but the stage was set.

In the same way that visionaries like Leonardo da Vinci painted masterpieces that transcended their time, my own experience in Iraq taught me that creativity knows no bounds. Leonardo, with his keen eye for detail and an insatiable appetite for understanding the world, unlocked the secrets of nature and artistry. He painted with the precision of a divine hand, creating works that continue to awe and inspire centuries later.

In these pages, we will journey through the realms of vision, drawing inspiration from both the extraordinary and the everyday. We will unravel the mysteries of how vision, whether in moments of foresight or boundless creativity, connects us to the divine. And most importantly, we will uncover the clues to unlocking your inner genius, where visions become realities and creativity flows as effortlessly as a master's brushstroke.

So let us delve deeper into the gift of vision—the power to see beyond the ordinary, to envision the extraordinary, and to harness creativity even in the most challenging of circumstances. Prepare to be amazed as we embark on a journey that will leave you with insights and tools to unlock your inner visionary genius. Certainly, let's continue and explore how the divine gift of vision connects us to boundless creativity and the genius of individuals like Leonardo da Vinci.

In the depths of Northern Iraq, where the stark reality of life and death played out daily, I marveled at the paradoxical nature of creativity. What was I capable of? What was my potential? And yet I didn't have an answer. It was as if the crucible of chaos had distilled the essence of inspiration, and under that pressure, creativity flowed like a river.

The novel I was crafting, set against a backdrop of uncertainty and tension, seemed to take on a life of its own. Characters sprung from the ether, their voices echoing in the silence of the night. Scenes unfolded effortlessly; each word infused with a vitality that I can only attribute to a source beyond myself. It was, I realized, a profound connection to the Divine—the very essence of GodMode.

Leonardo da Vinci, too, understood this connection intimately. His visionary genius wasn't merely the product of an agile mind; it was a manifestation of his insatiable curiosity and unyielding commitment to understanding the world around him. Leonardo's gift of vision went beyond artistry; it encompassed science, engineering, and a relentless quest for knowledge.

As I navigated the intricacies of my novel, I felt a kinship with Leonardo's tireless pursuit of detail and depth. His notebooks, brimming with sketches and observations, reveal a mind attuned to the subtlest nuances of the natural world. It was this unwavering attention to detail that allowed him to paint the *Mona Lisa's* enigmatic smile and design machines that foreshadowed the future.

Leonardo's genius teaches us that vision isn't limited to the realm of art alone. It's a force that transcends boundaries, inspiring innovation in fields as diverse as anatomy and engineering. It's the ability to see not only what is but also what could be—a testament to the boundless potential of the human spirit.

In your own life, have you ever experienced a moment of clarity, a vision that surpassed ordinary understanding? Perhaps it was a sudden insight into a complex problem, an idea that seemed to come from nowhere, or a glimpse of a future yet to unfold. These moments are not coincidences; they are the whispers of the Divine, urging you to tap into your inner genius.

We will explore how to cultivate and harness the gift of vision. We will delve into the practices of meditation and self-discovery, unlocking the latent powers of creativity within you. We will draw inspiration from Leonardo's relentless pursuit of knowledge, guiding you to become a visionary in your own right.

Prepare to embark on a journey where vision becomes a bridge between the ordinary and the extraordinary, where creativity flows like a mighty river and where the genius within you awakens to shape the world around you. As we unravel the secrets, you will discover that the divine spark of creativity resides not only in the realm of gods and geniuses but within your own soul.

So, dear reader, let us continue this exploration into the heart of creativity and vision with Leonardo da Vinci as our guide and inspiration. Together, we will unlock the extraordinary power that dwells within you. Certainly, let's delve into some of Leonardo da Vinci's lesser-known projects and draw inspiration from another remarkable artist.

As we navigate the corridors of Leonardo da Vinci's boundless genius, we uncover projects that stand as testaments to his insatiable curiosity and the breadth of his vision.

1. *The Anatomy of Genius:* Leonardo's fascination with the human body went far beyond his artistic endeavors. He embarked on a journey of dissection, seeking to unravel the mysteries of anatomy. His detailed sketches and meticulous notes, preserved in his notebooks, laid the foundation for our modern understanding of human anatomy.

2. *The Codex Atlanticus:* Leonardo's *Codex Atlanticus* is a collection of over a thousand pages of his thoughts, observations, and inventions. Within this treasure trove of knowledge, you'll find designs for flying machines, watercraft, and even a robotic knight. It's a testament to his visionary genius and his desire to push the boundaries of possibility.

3. *The Quest for Flight:* Long before the Wright brothers took to the skies, Leonardo was captivated by the dream of human flight. His sketches and designs for flying machines, including ornithopters and gliders, demonstrate his relentless pursuit of the extraordinary.

In my own journey, like many artists, I began expressing myself artistically at a young age. At the tender age of nine, I found solace and inspiration in the world of poetry. I penned verses that flowed from my heart, a glimpse into the boundless creativity that resides within us from the earliest of years. I even had the privilege of publishing one of my poems—a small but significant step on my path to self-expression.

To draw inspiration from another lesser-known artist, let's turn to the life and work of Amrita Sher-Gil, a trailblazing Indian painter. Like Leonardo, Amrita was driven by a profound sense of vision and a desire to express the depth of human experience through her art. Her vivid, emotive paintings not only captured the essence of her subjects but also transcended cultural boundaries, leaving a lasting impact on the art world.

In her short but impactful life, Amrita Sher-Gil became a beacon of artistic brilliance, demonstrating that true vision knows no borders. Her work resonated with a universal audience, underscoring the power of art to bridge gaps and evoke emotions that transcend language and culture.

Now as you journey through the pages, I invite you to reflect on your own moments of clarity and creativity, whether they occurred in childhood or adulthood. Embrace the inner artist that resides within you, for it is this creative spark that connects you to the divine.

The gift of vision transcends the ordinary, where extraordinary insights, artistic brilliance, and profound understanding converge.

Visionary insights

Throughout history, individuals have possessed the gift of vision—seeing things clearly when others faltered in the shadows of uncertainty.

One such visionary was Nikola Tesla, the brilliant inventor and engineer.

In the late nineteenth century, Tesla visualized a world powered by alternating current, a concept that would revolutionize electricity. Despite skepticism and challenges, his unwavering vision led to the development of AC power systems, which we rely on today.

Practical exercise 1: The Tesla Experiment: Embrace your inner visionary with the Tesla Experiment. Take a moment each day to visualize a future where your creative aspirations have been realized. Close your eyes and vividly imagine the details—what it feels like, the sights and sounds, the emotions. This exercise helps sharpen your visionary abilities and aligns your actions with your ultimate creative goals.

A few question to keep in mind:

1. *How did the Tesla Experiment exercise make you feel, both before and after trying it?*

2. *Describe any unexpected or surprising results or discoveries you encountered during the experiment.*

3. *Did you notice any changes in your thought patterns, energy levels, or overall mindset as a result of the exercise?*

4. *What aspects of Nikola Tesla's approach to creativity and problem-solving do you find most intriguing or inspiring?*

5. *Reflect on any parallels between Tesla's innovative mindset and your own approach to creativity.*

6. *How do you think embracing unconventional thinking, like Tesla did, can benefit your creative endeavors?*

7. *Did the exercise lead to any new ideas, projects, or insights that you plan to pursue further?*

8. *Share any challenges or obstacles you encountered during the exercise and how you overcame them.*

9. *Consider how incorporating similar creative practices into your daily routine could enhance your overall creativity and problem-solving abilities.*

10. *What long-term impact do you believe the Tesla Experiment exercise could have on your creative journey? Feel free to adapt these questions to suit your specific goals and intentions for the Tesla Experiment exercise.*

Artistic brilliance

Vision is often the cornerstone of artistic brilliance. Leonardo da Vinci, one of the greatest artists in history, was not only a painter but a visionary thinker. His ability to see beyond the surface of things allowed him to create masterpieces like the *Mona Lisa* and *The Last Supper*. Leonardo's relentless pursuit of excellence in art and science showcases the creative potential of a visionary mind.

Practical exercise 2: The Da Vinci Sketch: The Da Vinci Sketch exercise invites you to embrace your inner artist and visionary. Pick up a sketchbook or digital drawing tool and create a simple sketch each day. It doesn't need to be perfect—just a representation of something you envision or observe in your surroundings. This practice nurtures your artistic abilities and fosters a deeper connection to your creative vision.

Here are some questions for reflection and exploration after completing The Da Vinci Sketch exercise:

1. *How did creating your own Da Vinci-style sketch make you feel? Describe any emotions or thoughts that arose during the process.*

2. *What aspects of Leonardo da Vinci's approach to art and creativity did you find most inspiring or challenging while working on your sketch?*

3. *Reflect on the experience of blending different artistic elements—such as science, nature, and art—into your sketch. How did this interdisciplinary approach affect your creative process?*

4. *Describe any insights or new perspectives you gained about your own creative abilities while completing "The Da Vinci Sketch."*

5. *Were there any unexpected connections or patterns that emerged in your sketch, linking seemingly unrelated ideas or concepts?*

6. *Consider the idea of balance and harmony in your sketch. How did you achieve or struggle with achieving balance in your composition, both visually and conceptually?*

7. *Did the exercise lead to any new ideas or projects you'd like to pursue further? If so, what are they?*

8. *Reflect on how incorporating elements of Da Vinci's approach, such as curiosity and observation, into your daily life could enhance your creativity and problem-solving abilities.*

9. *Share any challenges or obstacles you encountered during the exercise and how you addressed them.*

10. *How do you envision applying the principles and lessons learned from "The Da Vinci Sketch" to your future creative endeavors? These questions can help you delve deeper into the insights and experiences gained from the exercise and guide your creative journey moving forward.*

Profound understanding

Vision also leads to profound understanding. Dr. Jane Goodall, renowned for her work with chimpanzees, possessed a unique vision of bridging the gap between humans and animals. Her pioneering research revealed the complexity of chimpanzee societies, shedding light on the interconnectedness of all life on earth.

Practical exercise 3: The Jane Goodall Connection: The Jane Goodall Connection exercise encourages you to connect with the natural world and develop a deeper understanding of the environment. Spend time in nature, whether it's a local park or a hike in the wilderness. Observe the intricacies of the natural world and contemplate your role in it. This exercise fosters a profound connection with the world around you, fueling your vision for a more harmonious and sustained future.

Here are some questions for reflection and exploration after completing "The Jane Goodall Connection" exercise:

1. *How did immersing yourself in Jane Goodall's world and work make you feel? Describe any emotions or thoughts that arose during the exercise.*

2. *Reflect on the idea of observing and understanding nature as emphasized by Jane Goodall. What did you learn from this exercise about the power of keen observation in creativity?*

3. *Consider Jane Goodall's deep connection with chimpanzees and her ability to communicate with them. How can empathy and connection with your subject matter enhance your creative process?*

4. *Describe any unexpected connections or insights that emerged during your exploration of Jane Goodall's life and work. Did you discover any parallels with your own creative journey?*

5. *How did the exercise influence your perspective on the environment, conservation, or the importance of protecting wildlife and their habitats?*

6. *Reflect on Jane Goodall's dedication and lifelong commitment to her work. How might maintaining such dedication and passion impact your own creative endeavors?*

7. *Were there any specific elements or aspects of Jane Goodall's story or methodology that resonated with you on a personal or creative level?*

8. *Share any challenges or obstacles you encountered during the exercise and how you addressed them.*

9. *Did this exercise lead to any new ideas, projects, or creative directions you'd like to pursue further? If so, what are they?*

10. *How do you envision incorporating the lessons and inspiration drawn from The Jane Goodall Connection into your future creative work and daily life? These questions can help you gain deeper insights from the exercise and inspire you to further integrate the principles and values exemplified by Jane Goodall into your creative journey.*

Moses and Martin Luther King Jr. are both iconic figures known for their powerful visions of justice, freedom, and equality. While their lives were separated by thousands of years, their unwavering commitment to their respective visions and the sacrifices they made are deeply resonant.

Moses and the promised land: Moses is perhaps best known for his role in leading the Israelites out of slavery in Egypt and guiding them through the wilderness toward the promised land. His vision was not only about physical liberation but also the promise of a better life for his people, characterized by freedom and self-determination. However, despite his dedication and the countless trials he faced during the arduous journey, Moses did not live to see the fulfillment of his vision. According to biblical accounts, he was able to glimpse the promised land from afar but was not permitted to enter it himself. This aspect of Moses' story illustrates the bittersweet nature of visionary leadership, where one's profound commitment to a cause may not always culminate in personal fulfillment.

Moses' vision can be analyzed in its core elements:

- *The quest for freedom:* At its heart, Moses' vision was about emancipation. He envisioned a future where his people were no longer enslaved and oppressed. This aspiration for freedom resonated deeply with the Israelites who yearned for liberation.

- *A land flowing with milk and honey:* The promised land symbolized abundance and prosperity. Moses' vision included a place where his people could thrive, build communities, and enjoy the fruits of their labor.
- *Guidance by divine principles:* Moses' vision was grounded in faith and divine guidance. He saw his role as a leader appointed by God, tasked with shepherding his people to a land where they could live according to the principles of justice and righteousness.
- *A legacy of resilience:* Moses' vision was transformative because it required resilience and unwavering commitment. His leadership was marked by perseverance in the face of adversity, and this resilience became a cornerstone of his vision.

Martin Luther King Jr. and the dream: Martin Luther King Jr., a prominent figure in the American Civil Rights Movement, is renowned for his vision of racial equality and social justice. His famous "I Have a Dream" speech, delivered during the March on Washington for Jobs and Freedom in 1963, remains an iconic moment in history. King's vision went beyond the immediate struggle for civil rights; it encompassed a future where individuals were judged by the content of their character rather than the color of their skin. He envisioned a society where equality and justice prevailed. Tragically, like Moses, Martin Luther King Jr. did not live to witness the full realization of his dream. He was assassinated in 1968, and many of the issues he fought for continued to be debated and challenged long after his passing. Nevertheless, his vision inspired a movement that led to significant changes in American society, including the Civil Rights Act of 1964 and the Voting Rights Act of 1965. King's vision can also be dissected into core elements:

- *Racial equality:* King's vision was clear in its call for racial equality. He articulated a future where individuals would be judged by their character rather than the color of their skin. This vision resonated with those who yearned for an end to racial discrimination.

- *Justice and civil rights:* King's vision extended beyond abstract ideals. He aimed to achieve tangible changes through civil rights legislation, equal access to opportunities, and an end to segregation.
- *Nonviolent resistance:* A fundamental element of King's vision was the practice of nonviolent resistance. He believed in the power of peaceful protest and civil disobedience as a means to achieve social change.
- *Inclusivity and unity:* King's vision emphasized unity among diverse communities and inclusivity. He envisioned a society where people of all backgrounds would come together to work toward a common goal.

Both Moses and Martin Luther King Jr. serve as powerful examples of individuals whose visions transcended their lifetimes. Their stories highlight the enduring impact that a clear and compelling vision can have on the course of history, even if the visionaries themselves do not live to see its complete realization. They remind us that true visionary leadership is not solely about personal achievement but about catalyzing change that extends beyond one's own lifetime, shaping the future for generations to come.

As we journey through, remember that this superpower is not exclusive to history's luminaries. It resides within each of us, waiting to be nurtured and unleashed. In the chapters ahead, we'll explore more stories, exercises, and insights that will empower you to harness your own gift of vision. Join me on this transformative path as we uncover the hidden realms of creativity, tap into the powers of vision, and awaken the creative giants within. Warmest wishes on your visionary journey.

As the chapter draws to a close, remember these words of wisdom:

> **The noblest pleasure is the joy of understanding. (Leonardo da Vinci)**

Every artist dips his brush in his soul and paints his own nature into his pictures. (Henry Ward Beecher)

Let these quotes serve as beacons of inspiration as we embark on this voyage of self-discovery and creativity. In the chapters ahead, you will uncover practical tools and insights to unlock your inner genius to see the world with fresh eyes and to harness "the gift of vision" to shape your destiny.

Are you ready to unleash the visionary within you? The journey has just begun, and the world of boundless creativity awaits. Embrace your gift of vision and let us together walk the path of artistic enlightenment.

2

The Art of Resilience

In the face of adversity, true strength emerges. Resilience is the power to endure and overcome life's challenges, and it is an art that can be mastered.

Resilience—the art of bouncing back from setbacks and adversity—is a quality that defines the human spirit. It's the unyielding determination to rise when life's storms threaten to break us, and it's a force that resides deep within each of us. In this chapter, we will explore "The Art of Resilience," a God superpower that empowers us to thrive in the face of adversity. As I reflect on my own journey, I'm reminded of the countless moments when resilience became not just a virtue but a lifeline. From the battlefield of Iraq to the unforgiving world of entertainment, resilience was the bedrock upon which I built my path. But my story is just one thread in the tapestry of resilience that weaves through human history. Consider the story of Louisa May Alcott, the beloved author of *Little Women*. Despite facing numerous rejections in her early career, she never let setbacks deter her. Her resilience was the guiding force that propelled her from obscurity to literary acclaim, and her words continue to inspire generations of readers. Now let's embark on a journey to understand the art of resilience and how to cultivate it in your own life. But before we dive deeper, let's pause for a moment of reflection:

Practical exercise 1: The Resilience Journal: Take out a notebook or open a digital document. Begin by jotting down three challenging moments in your life when you displayed resilience. These could be personal, professional, or even moments of inner struggle. For each of these moments, reflect on the following: *What was the adversity you faced?* How did you find the inner strength to overcome it? What lessons did you learn from these experiences? This journal will become a valuable tool in your journey to master the art of resilience. It will serve as a reminder of your own inner strength and provide insights that will guide you through life's challenges. As we delve deeper into this chapter, we will explore the principles of resilience, drawing inspiration from both historical figures and your own experiences. The art of resilience is not just about surviving; it's about thriving in the face of adversity. Let's unlock this superpower together and discover the boundless strength within.

Resilience, often born out of adversity, is the key to transforming doubt into unwavering belief. It's about finding the strength to persevere even when the world doubts your dreams. My journey from the military to the world of acting is a testament to the art of resilience and the power of self-belief.

1. The look of an artist: Leaving the army to pursue a life in the arts was met with skepticism from many. The doubts, both internal and external, were like shadows that threatened to obscure the path ahead. I had no road map for success or how I was gonna survive. Yet amid the uncertainty, there was a glimmer of hope. One noncommissioned officer (NCO) from another company saw something beyond the uniform. He recognized the potential for a different kind of artistry—an artistry of storytelling and emotion. He saw "the look of an artist" in me, even when I couldn't draw a straight line. It was a spark of belief that set my journey in motion.

Grief, like a storm, has the power to shatter our world into a thousand pieces. I have lost several beloved family members over the years. Each one's absence unreplaceable. When my beloved mother lost her battle to cancer, it felt as if the sun had set on my life forever. The weight of sorrow was overwhelming. The pain unmeasurable. Yet within nine months of that heart-wrenching loss, I found myself in the spotlight, starring in a national NFL commercial for one of the biggest Thursday night football games in history. It was a testament to the resilience that can emerge from the darkest of hours.

My story, like those of countless others, underscores the transformative power of resilience. It's about refusing to be defined by circumstances and pushing through doubt and adversity to achieve the extraordinary. Resilience isn't about denying the challenges we face; it's about rising above them, using doubt as a stepping stone to belief.

In the same way, consider the life of Maya Angelou, a towering figure in literature and civil rights. She faced a childhood marred by trauma and discrimination. Yet her journey from a silenced victim to a powerful voice for change exemplifies the art of resilience. Maya's words, like beacons of hope, continue to inspire and uplift, reminding us that we have the power to transcend our circumstances.

Now let's dive deeper into the art of resilience and explore practical exercises to cultivate this superpower in your own life:

Practical exercise: The Resilience Manifesto: Create a list of affirmations that encapsulate your resilience. These could be short phrases or sentences that remind you of your inner strength, your ability to overcome doubt, and your unwavering belief in your dreams. For example: "I am resilient in the face of doubt," "I turn adversity into opportunity," "My belief in myself is unshakeable."

Here are some questions for the "Resilience Manifesto" exercise:

1. *What are some personal challenges or setbacks you've faced in your life? How did you respond to these challenges?*

2. *Reflect on a time when you demonstrated resilience. What was the situation, and how did you overcome it? What did you learn from that experience?*

3. *In the face of adversity, what strategies or coping mechanisms have helped you maintain resilience? Are there specific practices or rituals that ground you during tough times?*

4. *Think about a creative project or goal you're currently pursuing. How can you apply the principles of resilience to overcome obstacles and keep moving forward?*

5. *What role does self-belief play in resilience? How can you nurture and strengthen your self-belief in creative endeavors?*

6. *Resilience often involves adapting to change. Can you recall a situation where you had to pivot or adapt your creative approach to achieve your desired outcome?*

7. *Consider the support systems and relationships in your life. How do they contribute to your resilience? Are there individuals or communities that have been instrumental in helping you bounce back from challenges?*

8. *Think about the vision you have for your creative journey. How does resilience tie into your long-term goals and aspirations? How can you stay resilient in pursuit of your creative dreams?*

9. *Create your own "Resilience Manifesto" by listing key principles or affirmations that resonate with you. How can you incorporate these principles into your daily life and creative pursuits?*

These questions are designed to help you explore the concept of resilience and how it applies to your creative journey, drawing inspiration from both your personal experiences and the stories of visionary leaders.

Keep this manifesto close, refer to it daily, and let it be a source of inspiration and motivation as you navigate the challenges of life. As we journey further into "The Art of Resilience," remember the words of Maya Angelou:

> You may encounter many defeats, but you must not be defeated. In fact, it may be necessary to encounter the defeats, so you can know who you are, what you can rise from, how you can still come out of it.

In the face of doubt and adversity, you have the power to rise, to turn defeat into victory, and to craft your own narrative of resilience. Let the art of resilience be your guiding light on this transformative journey.

In the world of cinema, Chadwick Boseman was a shining star—a true embodiment of resilience and unwavering belief. His portrayal of iconic figures like Jackie Robinson and T'Challa in Marvel's *Black Panther* was not just a testament to his talent but a reflection of his commitment to artistry and the human spirit.

Around 2014, I had the privilege of meeting Chadwick Boseman after church in Los Angeles. Even then I could see the potential radiating from him, a potential that would eventually propel him to the pinnacle of Hollywood. His portrayal of Jackie Robinson in *42* was marked by a profound dignity that transcended the screen. It was clear that he was destined for greatness, destined to be one of the top Black male actors of our time. In that moment, I felt compelled to share some simple advice with Chadwick. It wasn't advice born of arrogance but of absolute encouragement and love for his potential. I urged him to keep believing in his own resilience, to never waver in the face of adversity, and to use his immense talent to inspire generations. Little did I know how profoundly those words would resonate in the years to come.

Chadwick Boseman's journey is a poignant example of resilience in the face of unimaginable challenges. While the world celebrated his on-screen triumphs, behind the scenes, he was waging a private battle with cancer. Despite the physical and emotional toll, he continued to work, to create, and to inspire. He completed films like *Ma Rainey's Black Bottom* and *Da 5 Bloods* while battling the very disease that would eventually claim his life.

His unwavering commitment to his craft and his unyielding belief in the power of storytelling were a testament to the art of resilience. Chadwick didn't just act; he embodied the indomitable spirit of characters who defied the odds, characters like Jackie Robinson and T'Challa. Chadwick Boseman's legacy reminds us that resilience is not limited to the characters we portray on screen. It's a quality that defines the human experience, an art that transcends the boundaries of entertainment.

It's the ability to face adversity with grace, to transform challenges into opportunities, and to leave an indelible mark on the world. As we continue our exploration remember the words of Chadwick Boseman himself: *"The struggles along the way are only meant to shape you for your purpose."*

In the face of doubt, adversity, and loss, you have the power to shape your own purpose and rise above life's challenges. Let Chadwick's resilience and unwavering belief inspire you on this journey. As we delve deeper into the art of resilience, let his legacy remind us that the human spirit is capable of extraordinary feats when fueled by resilience and belief.

The Harlem Renaissance

During a time of racial discrimination and segregation, the Harlem Renaissance was a cultural and artistic explosion that brought African American art, music, literature, and intellectualism to the forefront. Visionaries like Langston Hughes, Zora Neale Hurston, and Duke Ellington used their creativity to challenge the status quo, to uplift their communities, and to prove that resilience could lead to artistic brilliance. In the midst of this collective resurgence, Langston Hughes penned a poem that still resonates today:

> *Hold fast to dreams,*
> *For if dreams die,*
> *Life is a broken-winged bird*
> *That cannot fly.*

It's crucial to recognize that resilience is not a solitary endeavor; it's a shared journey that can uplift entire communities.

Practical exercise 3: The Resilience Circle: Consider forming a resilience circle—a supportive group of friends, family, or peers who share the journey of resilience with you. This circle will serve as a source of encouragement, inspiration, and shared experiences. In your first meeting, discuss your individual challenges and goals for resilience. Share stories of artists and figures who have inspired you, like Chadwick Boseman or the Harlem Renaissance visionaries. Commit to supporting each other in times of doubt and celebrating each other's successes. Together, you'll create a network of resilience that can endure even the toughest of storms.

Remember that resilience is a force that connects us, not only to our inner strength but also to the strength of our communities. Just as the Harlem Renaissance artists used their creativity to defy oppression and inspire change, you too have the power to create ripples of resilience that can transform the world around you.

Objective: This exercise aims to create a supportive and resilient community among participants, fostering a sense of shared purpose and mutual encouragement in their creative journeys.

Instructions:

1. ***Gather a group:*** Form a small group of individuals who share a common interest in creativity, whether it's writing, art, music, or any other creative endeavor. This can be done virtually or in person.

2. ***Define the purpose:*** Start by discussing the purpose of the Resilience Circle. Emphasize that it's a safe and confidential space where participants can share their creative challenges and support each other in building resilience.

3. ***Set the frequency:*** Decide on the frequency of your Resilience Circle meetings. It could be weekly, biweekly, or monthly, depending on the group's availability.

4. ***Rotating facilitator:*** Designate a rotating facilitator for each meeting. This person will lead the discussions and activities for that session.

5. ***Sharing challenges:*** In each meeting, one participant shares a creative challenge or setback they've encountered recently. This could be a writer's block, self-doubt, a rejection, or any obstacle they're facing in their creative journey.

6. ***Group discussion:*** After sharing the challenge, open the floor for group discussion. Encourage participants to offer suggestions, insights, and strategies to overcome the challenge. This is a collaborative brainstorming session.

7. ***Resilience strategies:*** Discuss resilience strategies that can be applied to the shared challenge. Explore how self-belief, adaptability, support systems, and other resilience principles can help in the specific situation.

8. ***Action steps:*** Together, create a list of actionable steps that the participant can take to address their challenge. These steps should align with the resilience strategies discussed.

9. ***Accountability:*** At the next meeting, check in on the progress made by the participant who shared their challenge in the previous session. Celebrate their successes and provide additional support if needed.

10. ***Rotating challenges:*** Continue rotating challenges and facilitating roles in subsequent meetings, ensuring that each participant has the opportunity to seek support and contribute to the resilience of the group.

11. ***Optional exercises:*** Occasionally, incorporate creative exercises or prompts into your Resilience Circle meetings to spark creativity and strengthen participants' resilience.

12. ***Reflection:*** Periodically, take time to reflect on how the Resilience Circle has impacted each participant's creative journey. Share stories of resilience and growth that have emerged from these meetings.

Benefits:

- The Resilience Circle creates a sense of community and shared purpose among creative individuals.
- It offers a platform for participants to openly discuss challenges and receive practical advice.
- By focusing on resilience principles, participants learn how to navigate creative obstacles more effectively.
- The rotating facilitator role promotes leadership and communication skills.
- The accountability aspect encourages participants to take actionable steps toward their creative goals. Remember that the Resilience Circle is not just about problem-solving but also about building a network of support and resilience in the creative process.

Now let us turn to another artist whose story of resilience has inspired generations, Vincent van Gogh.

Vincent van Gogh: Often misunderstood and underappreciated during his lifetime, Vincent van Gogh faced countless setbacks and personal struggles. Yet his resilience and unrelenting dedication to his art led to a body of work that continues to captivate the world.

His vibrant, emotionally charged paintings, like *Starry Night*, are a testament to the transformative power of art and the human spirit. Van Gogh's journey reminds us that resilience is not always a shield against adversity; sometimes it's a beacon that guides us through the darkest of nights. His story is a testament to the enduring nature of creativity and the indomitable spirit of artists who refuse to be defined by doubt or setbacks.

Let the resilience of the Harlem Renaissance and Vincent van Gogh inspire you to keep dreaming, to keep creating, and to keep believing in your own journey. Remember that like these artists, your resilience can lead to moments of artistic brilliance that transcend the limitations of doubt and adversity.

In the annals of history, there are stories of resilience that defy imagination, stories that remind us of the incredible strength that resides within the human spirit. One such story is that of General Roscoe Robinson Jr.

General Roscoe Robinson Jr.: Born in 1928, General Robinson was a trailblazer in the US military, and his journey was one of unwavering resilience. In the face of immense racial discrimination and the formidable challenges of being an African American soldier, he shattered barriers and rose through the ranks to become the first four-star general in the US Army.

General Robinson's journey was marked by the deep-seated belief that resilience and perseverance could overcome even the most entrenched obstacles. His path to leadership was not an easy one; it was filled with moments of doubt, adversity, and discrimination. Yet he continued to serve his country with honor, rising through the ranks one step at a time. His resilience was not just a personal triumph; it was a victory for the entire community of African American soldiers who aspired to serve their country with dignity and equality. His achievements opened doors and shattered ceilings, proving that resilience could rewrite the narrative of history.

Practical exercise 4: The Resilience Tribute: Research and share the stories of remarkable individuals like General Roscoe Robinson Jr., who have exhibited extraordinary resilience in the face of adversity. Discuss their journeys with your resilience circle or within your community. Consider hosting a resilience tribute event where you celebrate and honor the achievements of these resilient figures. Share their stories and discuss how their resilience can serve as a source of inspiration in your own lives. This exercise will not only deepen your understanding of resilience but also pay tribute to those who have blazed trails before us. As we reflect on the incredible story of General Robinson and the resilience of countless others, remember that resilience is not just a personal attribute; it's a force that can inspire change on a grand scale. In our collective resilience, we find the strength to overcome societal challenges and redefine the limits of what is possible.

Resilience isn't confined to a single era or generation; it's a timeless quality that transcends boundaries. To appreciate the enduring nature of resilience, we need look no further than the life of Frederick Douglass.

Frederick Douglass: Born into slavery in the early 1800s, Frederick Douglass defied the brutal shackles of bondage to become one of the most prominent abolitionists, writers, and orators in American history. His journey from a life of servitude to one of leadership and activism is a testament to the indomitable spirit of resilience. Frederick Douglass recognized that literacy was the key to his freedom, and with unwavering determination, he taught himself to read and write. His thirst for knowledge and justice fueled his escape from slavery, and he went on to become a powerful advocate for the abolition of slavery and the rights of African Americans. Through his eloquent speeches and writings, including his autobiography, *Narrative of the Life of Frederick Douglass, an American Slave,* he challenged the very foundations of slavery and discrimination. His resilience in the face of unimaginable adversity not only reshaped his own destiny but also the course of American history.

Practical exercise 5: The Resilience Reflection: Take time to reflect on your own journey of resilience. Write a letter to yourself or create a personal essay that chronicles the moments in your life when you displayed resilience. Share your reflections with your resilience circle or a trusted friend. Consider what fueled your resilience, the lessons you learned, and how those experiences have shaped your character. Recognize the strengths you've developed through resilience and how they continue to guide you on your path. As we draw inspiration from the life of Frederick Douglass and the countless others who have exhibited resilience, remember that your own journey of resilience is a testament to your inner strength. It's a journey that shapes not only your life but also the lives of those around you.

Here are some questions for the "Resilience Reflection" exercise:

1. *Reflect on the creative challenge or setback you shared during the Resilience Circle. What were the specific obstacles you faced?*

2. *Did you apply any of the resilience strategies discussed in the Resilience Circle to address your challenge? If so, which strategies were most helpful, and why?*

3. *Describe any positive changes or progress you've observed in your creative journey since seeking support from the Resilience Circle.*

4. *Have you encountered any new challenges or setbacks since the last Resilience Circle meeting? If yes, what*

are they, and how do you plan to approach them with resilience?

5. *How has the support and feedback from the Resilience Circle influenced your mindset and approach to creative challenges?*

6. *Are there any new insights or strategies you've gained from the Resilience Circle discussions that you intend to incorporate into your creative practice moving forward?*

7. *Reflect on your overall experience in the Resilience Circle. What have been the most valuable aspects of participating in this supportive community?*

8. *Have you found that discussing challenges openly and seeking input from others has helped you become more resilient in your creative endeavors? If so, in what ways?*

9. *How do you envision your creative journey evolving in the future, knowing that you have a support system in place to address challenges with resilience?*

10. *In what ways can you contribute to the growth and resilience of your fellow Resilience Circle members? How can you continue to foster a supportive creative community?*

11. *Share any specific goals or creative projects you're currently working on and how resilience principles will play a role in achieving them.*

12. *Finally, take a moment to express gratitude for the support and camaraderie of your Resilience Circle members. What are you thankful for in this creative journey together? These questions are designed to facilitate*

self-reflection and encourage participants to assess their growth and resilience in the context of their creative pursuits and the support received from the Resilience Circle.

Human existence resilience is the thread that binds our stories, the force that propels us forward, and the artistry that transforms adversity into opportunity. We have journeyed through the lives of remarkable individuals, from Chadwick Boseman's unwavering belief in his own potential to General Roscoe Robinson Jr.'s unrelenting rise through the ranks of the US Army.

We've seen how the Harlem Renaissance and Vincent van Gogh turned doubt and adversity into artistic brilliance and how Frederick Douglass used the power of knowledge to shatter the chains of slavery. Resilience is not a solitary endeavor; it's a shared journey that connects us to a greater purpose and to the collective strength of communities and generations. It's an art that transcends time, a force that uplifts us when doubt and adversity threaten to dim our spirits. It's the indomitable spirit that reminds us that we are capable of achieving greatness no matter the odds stacked against us. Remember that your journey—like those of the artists, leaders, and visionaries we've encountered—is a testament to your inner strength.

It's a journey that shapes not only your life but also the lives of those around you. Resilience is not just about surviving; it's about thriving, about using doubt and adversity as stepping stones to reach new heights. In the chapters to come, we will delve deeper into the strategies, tools, and insights that can help you cultivate and harness the superpower of resilience in your own life.

We will continue to draw inspiration from artists, leaders, and individuals who have harnessed this force to create lasting change and transform their worlds. Remember the words of Maya Angelou:

> *You may encounter many defeats, but you must not be defeated. In fact, it may be necessary to encounter the defeats, so you can know who you are, what you can rise from, how you can still come out of it.*

In the face of doubt and adversity, remember that you have the power to rise, to turn defeats into victories, and to craft your own narrative of resilience. Let the art of resilience be your guiding light on this transformative journey.

3

The Creative Spark

In the heart of every individual, there exists a spark, a divine gift that sets our imagination ablaze. This is the gift of creativity—a force that shapes our world, fuels our passions, and brings forth the genius within.

Creativity is the wellspring of human innovation and expression. It's the ability to envision the extraordinary, to connect disparate ideas, and to give birth to something entirely new. In this chapter, we journey into the realm of "The Creative Spark," a God superpower that resides within each of us. From the earliest cave paintings to the latest technological marvels, creativity has been the driving force behind human progress. It's what enables us to turn raw materials into art, to weave words into stories, and to transform thoughts into inventions. But creativity is not limited to artists and inventors; it's a gift that belongs to all of us, waiting to be unlocked. Throughout history, countless individuals have harnessed the power of the creative spark to change the course of humanity. They've painted masterpieces, composed symphonies, written manifestos, and designed innovations that defy the bounds of possibility. And in each of their stories, we find clues to unlocking our own creative genius.

Exercise 1: The Creative Journal: Start a creative journal to capture your thoughts, ideas, and moments of inspiration. This journal will become a repository for your creative sparks, a place to nurture your imagination. Carry it with you throughout the day, jotting down any ideas or insights that come to you no matter how small they may seem. Remember that creativity is not a finite resource; it's a wellspring that flows endlessly. Your creative journal will become a treasure trove of ideas and concepts, a testament to the boundless potential of your imagination.

Here are some questions for the Creative Journal exercise:

1. *How has the practice of keeping a creative journal impacted your creative process and overall mindset?*

2. *Describe a recent entry in your creative journal. What inspired you to write or draw about that particular topic or experience?*

3. *Have you noticed any patterns or recurring themes in your journal entries that provide insights into your creative interests or challenges?*

4. *Reflect on the goals you've set for your creative journey. How do you use your creative journal to track progress toward these goals?*

5. *Are there any specific creative exercises or prompts from your journal that have sparked new ideas or breakthroughs in your work?*

6. *Explore how self-reflection in your creative journal has influenced your self-belief and confidence in your abilities as a creative individual.*

7. *Have you encountered moments of self-doubt or creative block? How does your journal serve as a tool to navigate and overcome these challenges?*

8. *Consider the importance of documenting your creative journey. What role does your journal play in preserving memories and insights from your creative experiences?*

9. *Share a favorite journal entry where you explored a new technique, idea, or artistic expression. What did you learn from that exploration?*

10. *Reflect on the power of journaling as a source of resilience in your creative life. How has it helped you bounce back from setbacks or setbacks?*

11. *Are there specific journal entries that you revisit for inspiration during moments of low motivation or creative fatigue?*

12. *How can you further enhance your creative journaling practice to support your ongoing creative growth and resilience? The purpose of these questions is to encourage individuals to reflect on the impact of their creative journaling practice, its role in nurturing resilience, and its contribution to their creative journey.*

Have you ever felt that surge of inspiration, that moment when your ideas seem unstoppable? I named my Zazzle store "Unlimited1" because I truly believe that pairing my ideas with AI art is an unbeatable combination. Even during the lockdown, when the world seemed to come to a halt, creativity continued to flow. I had a song burning in my mind, lyrics ready, but it took time to get the hook just right. Eventually, I found a talented singer Marcello Vieria, and we collaborated to bring "Southern Outlaw" to life. It was a team effort, and the result was beyond expectations. The song charted internationally and even made its way onto the radio in the UK. To this day, it remains a staple in my workout playlist. The story of "Southern Outlaw" exemplifies how creativity knows no boundaries. It can thrive even in the most challenging circumstances, like during a worldwide lockdown. This journey showcases how collaboration can amplify the creative spark, turning a simple idea into a masterpiece.

Practical exercise 2: The Collaborative Canvas: Reach out to a fellow artist, writer, or creator and embark on a collaborative project. It could be a song, a piece of artwork, a short story, or any endeavor that excites your creative spirits.

The key to successful collaboration is openness and shared vision. Collaborators bring diverse perspectives and skills to the table, enriching the creative process. Embrace the unique strengths of each contributor and watch as your combined creative sparks ignite into something extraordinary. As we remember that creativity thrives not just in isolation but in the fertile soil of collaboration and shared imagination, here are some questions for the "Collaborative Canvas" exercise:

1. *Describe your experience working on the collaborative canvas with your creative partner(s). What emotions or thoughts did this collaborative process evoke?*

2. *How did the collaborative canvas exercise challenge your creative boundaries or encourage you to explore new ideas and techniques?*

3. *Reflect on the final collaborative artwork. What aspects of your partner's contribution did you find most inspiring or surprising?*

4. *Did you encounter any creative conflicts or differences in perspective during the collaboration? How were these resolved, and what did you learn from the experience?*

5. *Consider the concept of synergy in collaboration. In what ways did the collaborative canvas result in a final artwork that was greater than the sum of its parts?*

6. *Explore the idea of trust in creative collaboration. How did you and your partner(s) establish trust in each other's creative choices and contributions?*

7. *Reflect on the balance between individual expression and collective creativity in the collaborative canvas project. How did you navigate this balance effectively?*

8. *Share any insights you gained about communication and effective collaboration through this exercise. What communication strategies proved most beneficial?*

9. *Consider the role of compromise in creative partnerships. Were there moments where compromise led to unexpected creative breakthroughs?*

10. *Reflect on the value of feedback and critique within the collaborative process. How did constructive feedback from your partner(s) enhance the final artwork?*

11. *Describe any personal or creative growth you experienced as a result of this collaboration. Did it challenge your assumptions or expand your creative horizons?*

12. *Finally, contemplate the potential for future collaborative projects. How can you apply the lessons learned from this exercise to future creative partnerships and endeavors?*

These questions are designed to promote self-reflection and encourage individuals to explore the dynamics of creative collaboration, highlighting the role of trust, communication, and growth in the process.

Like "Southern Outlaw," your own creative endeavors can reach heights you may never have imagined. Join me as we continue to explore the boundless depths of the creative spark—a force that knows no limits, that defies constraints, and that connects us to the endless possibilities of the human imagination.

But creativity is a universal force that transcends boundaries and can shape the lives of celebrated creators as well. Take, for instance, the incomparable story of Steve Jobs. Steve Jobs, a name synonymous with innovation and creativity, revolutionized the world of technology with his vision and imagination. As the cofounder of Apple Inc., he brought us iconic products like the iPhone, iPad, and Macintosh. Yet it's important to note that Steve Jobs didn't start his journey as a tech mogul. In his early years, he explored diverse creative pursuits, including calligraphy, Eastern spirituality, and backpacking through India. These experiences, seemingly unrelated to technology, played a pivotal role in shaping his unique perspective. Steve's fascination with calligraphy, for instance, later influenced the typography and fonts used in Apple's products. His exposure to Eastern philosophies and spirituality instilled in him a deep appreciation for simplicity and elegance in design, principles that would become hallmarks of Apple's products.

His journey from creative exploration to technological innovation is a testament to the transformative power of the creative spark. It reminds us that creativity isn't confined to a single field; it's a dynamic force that can bridge seemingly unrelated domains and lead to groundbreaking ideas.

Let us also delve into the story of a lesser-known artist, Clara Peeters, who, like Steve Jobs, demonstrated the universality of the creative spark. Clara was a seventeenth-century Flemish painter known for her still-life paintings. In a time when women artists faced significant barriers, Clara's work shone brightly. Her meticulous attention to detail and exquisite rendering of objects in her still lifes captivated viewers. Clara's art not only transcended the limitations of her era but also showed how creativity could elevate the ordinary to the extraordinary. Her journey is a reminder that creativity knows no gender, no era, and no boundaries. Clara Peeters harnessed her creative spark to bring beauty to the world through her art, proving that artistic brilliance can emerge from unexpected sources.

Practical exercise 3: The Clara Peeters Challenge: Inspired by Clara Peeters' ability to elevate the everyday, take up the Clara Peeters Challenge. Choose an ordinary object or scene from your daily life—a cup of coffee, a bouquet of flowers, or a street corner. Create a piece of art or write a description that captures the essence and beauty of this ordinary subject. This exercise encourages you to see the world with fresh eyes, just as Clara did with her still lifes. It's a testament to how the creative spark can transform the mundane into something extraordinary.

Here are some questions for the Clara Peeters Challenge exercise:

1. *Reflect on your experience recreating a Clara Peeters artwork. What aspects of her style or technique did you find most challenging or intriguing?*

2. *How did studying and attempting to recreate Peeters' work deepen your appreciation for her as an artist? What did you discover about her unique approach to still-life painting?*

3. *Describe the process of selecting a specific Clara Peeters painting to recreate. What drew you to that particular artwork, and did it pose any specific creative challenges?*

4. *Explore the concept of artistic homage. In what ways did your recreation pay tribute to Clara Peeters' legacy while also allowing for your own creative interpretation?*

5. *Reflect on the materials and techniques used in your recreation. How did these aspects influence your understanding of Peeters' craft and the era in which she worked?*

6. *Share any moments of creative discovery or breakthroughs you experienced while working on the Clara Peeters Challenge. Did it lead to any new insights or perspectives in your own artistic practice?*

7. *Consider the historical and cultural context of Clara Peeters' time. How did her work reflect the society and values of the Dutch Golden Age, and did you incorporate any of these elements into your recreation?*

8. *Reflect on the role of attention to detail in both Peeters' original artwork and your recreation. How did this exercise sharpen your eye for detail and precision in your creative work?*

9. *Explore the significance of preserving and celebrating the artistic contributions of historical women artists like Clara Peeters. What impact does this have on contemporary art and gender equality in the arts?*

10. *Describe any personal or artistic growth you experienced as a result of the Clara Peeters Challenge. How might this exercise influence your future artistic endeavors or appreciation of art history?*

11. *Finally, contemplate the value of art challenges and exercises in enhancing your creativity and knowledge of art history. Are there other artists or time periods you'd like to explore through similar challenges in the future?*

These questions aim to stimulate reflection on the Clara Peeters Challenge, encouraging participants to delve into the historical and artistic context while also considering the broader impact of such exercises on their creative journeys.

Consider the current AI revolution, a testament to how technology and creativity can merge in unexpected ways. The emergence of AI-generated humor, with AI characters delivering original funny short stories, has taken the world by storm. In my own podcast, *Tales That Tickle*, I've explored this innovative blend of technology and humor. AI characters come to life, delivering uproarious stories that leave listeners in stitches. The ability to craft humor and wit through artificial intelligence showcases how creativity knows no bounds, transcending traditional boundaries and opening new frontiers in comedy.

Let's draw inspiration from history once more, this time from the lives of two remarkable individuals who wielded their creative sparks to reshape the world.

Marie Curie: The Radiant Visionary: In the early twentieth century, amidst a world dominated by men, Marie Curie emerged as a beacon of scientific innovation. Her groundbreaking work in radioactivity led to the discovery of two elements, polonium and radium. Yet her creative spark extended beyond the laboratory. During World War I, Curie used her scientific expertise to develop mobile x-ray units known as "Little Curies." These units revolutionized battlefield medicine, allowing doctors to diagnose injuries quickly and accurately. Her vision and creativity not only advanced science but also saved countless lives on the frontlines.

Bob Ross: The Joyful Visionary: In the realm of art, Bob Ross is celebrated for his soothing voice, charismatic presence, and the creation of *The Joy of Painting*. His vision was simple yet profound: to make art accessible and enjoyable for everyone. With his distinctive wet-on-wet painting technique, he encouraged individuals to pick up a brush and create landscapes filled with "happy little trees" and "fluffy clouds."

Bob Ross' vision transcended the canvas. His gentle approach to teaching and his ability to convey the joy of creation through art continue to inspire countless individuals to tap into their own creative sparks, finding solace and fulfillment in the act of painting.

Practical exercise 4: The Curie-Ross Connection: Take inspiration from the Curie-Ross Connection. Explore a field or discipline that is completely new to you. Just as Marie Curie ventured into battlefield medicine and Bob Ross encouraged everyone to paint, try your hand at something unfamiliar. Embrace the joy of learning and creation in a different realm, unlocking fresh perspectives and kindling your creative spark.

Here are some questions for the Curie-Ross Connection exercise:

1. *Reflect on your experience during the Curie-Ross Connection exercise flow. Did the exchange of creative ideas and inspiration with your partner(s) enhance your own creative process?*

2. *Describe the creative project or piece you worked on in collaboration with your partner(s). What was the central theme or concept, and how did you approach it collectively?*

3. *Explore the dynamic between science and art in the Curie-Ross Connection flow. Did you draw inspiration from both Marie Curie's scientific contributions and Bob Ross' artistic influence?*

4. *Share any challenges or obstacles you encountered during the collaborative project. How did you and your partner(s) overcome these challenges, and what did you learn from the experience?*

5. *Reflect on the blending of two seemingly disparate fields—Science and Art—in your collaborative work. How did this interdisciplinary approach influence the final outcome and message of your project?*

6. *Consider the theme of innovation and risk-taking in the creative process as exemplified by Marie Curie's pioneering research and Bob Ross's groundbreaking art career. How did you incorporate elements of innovation into your project?*

7. *Describe any moments of creative synergy or unexpected discoveries that emerged during the Curie-Ross Connection exercise. Did your collaboration lead to new ideas or perspectives you hadn't considered before?*

8. *Reflect on the role of inspiration in creative work. How did Marie Curie's dedication to science and Bob's influence on music inspire you and your partner(s) to push creative boundaries?*

9. *Explore the concept of creative expression as a means of honoring and celebrating the achievements of historical figures like Curie and Ross. In what ways did your project pay tribute to their legacies?*

10. *Consider the impact of collaboration on your own creative journey. How might the lessons learned from the Curie-Ross Connection exercise influence your future artistic endeavors or interdisciplinary projects?*

11. *Finally, contemplate the value of cross-disciplinary collaborations in fostering creativity and innovation. Are there other historical figures or fields of study you'd like to explore through similar collaborative exercises in the future?*

These questions are designed to encourage reflection on the Curie-Ross Connection exercise, emphasizing the intersection of science and art, the power of collaboration, and the role of inspiration in creative endeavors.

Here are some cool facts on optimizing creativity:

1. *Diverse experiences boost creativity:* Engaging in a variety of experiences, even seemingly unrelated ones, can enhance creativity. Steve Jobs' calligraphy studies, for example, influenced the design of Apple's fonts.

2. *Positive emotions inspire creativity:* Experiencing positive emotions, like joy and curiosity, can foster creativity. This is why brainstorming sessions often encourage a fun and relaxed atmosphere.

3. *Sleep enhances creativity:* Quality sleep plays a crucial role in creativity. During REM sleep, your brain consolidates information and makes connections, leading to creative insights upon waking.

4. *Mindfulness meditation unleashes creativity:* Mindfulness practices can help calm the mind and remove mental barriers, allowing creative thoughts to flow more freely.

5. *Embracing failure fuels creativity:* Many creative breakthroughs come after multiple failures. Edison famously said, "I have not failed. I've just found ten thousand ways that won't work," in his pursuit of the light bulb.

6. *Travel expands creativity:* Experiencing different cultures and environments can stimulate creativity. Exposure to new perspectives and ideas while traveling can lead to novel insights.

7. ***Solitude spurs creativity:*** Spending time alone can boost creativity as it allows for deep thinking and self-reflection. Many great writers and artists have valued solitude for their creative processes.

8. ***Exercise enhances cognitive function:*** Regular physical activity can improve cognitive function, including creativity. Exercise increases blood flow to the brain, promoting clarity and innovative thinking.

9. ***Limiting distractions boosts focus:*** Minimizing distractions, such as turning off notifications, can improve concentration and provide a conducive environment for creative work.

10. ***Cross-disciplinary collaboration sparks ideas:*** Collaborating with individuals from diverse fields can lead to innovative solutions. Combining different expertise often results in unique and creative solutions to complex problems.

11. ***Nature nurtures creativity:*** Spending time in natural settings, such as forests or parks, has been shown to enhance creativity and problem-solving abilities.

12. ***Creative habits foster consistency:*** Developing creative habits, like daily writing or drawing, can help maintain a steady flow of creative ideas over time.

13. ***Challenging assumptions drives creativity:*** Questioning long-held assumptions and challenging the status quo can lead to groundbreaking innovations.

14. ***Positive feedback encourages creativity:*** Constructive feedback and encouragement from mentors and peers can

motivate individuals to explore and expand their creative abilities.

15. ***Creativity can be cultivated:*** While some may possess a natural flair for creativity, it can be developed and nurtured through practice, exploration, and a willingness to take risks.

Remember, creativity is a dynamic and limitless force within you. By embracing these facts and incorporating creative practices into your life, you can optimize your creative potential and unlock new realms of imagination and innovation.

Dreams and the surreal: Salvador Dalí, the famous surrealist artist, often claimed that his outlandish and surreal paintings were inspired by his dreams. His ability to tap into the absurd and dream-like was a testament to the creative potential of the subconscious mind. Dalí's iconic works, such as *The Persistence of Memory*, transport viewers to a surreal world where time seems to melt away.

Mistakes and accidents: Post-it notes, those ubiquitous sticky pieces of paper, were invented by Spencer Silver while he was trying to create a superstrong adhesive. Instead, he accidentally created a weak adhesive that became the foundation for a multibillion-dollar product. This happy accident, which began as a mistake, revolutionized the way we leave reminders and notes for ourselves.

Necessity and scarcity: During World War II, rationing led to the scarcity of materials like nylon. In response, women began drawing lines up the back of their legs, giving birth to the fashion trend of nylon stockings. This unexpected style statement emerged from the constraints of wartime scarcity, demonstrating how creativity can flourish when necessity drives innovation.

Mental health and struggles: Vincent van Gogh's masterpieces, like *Starry Night*, were created during times of mental turmoil. His brushwork and use of color were profoundly influenced by his emotional state, demonstrating that creativity can arise from inner struggles. Van Gogh's art has left an indelible mark on the world, showcasing the raw beauty of the human experience.

Children's imagination: Dr. Seuss, the beloved author of whimsical children's books, often credited his creativity to thinking like a child. His books, such as *The Cat in the Hat* and *Green Eggs and Ham*, embraced playful language and vivid illustrations, captivating both children and adults. Dr. Seuss' imaginative storytelling has inspired generations to nurture their inner child and embrace the power of whimsy.

Nature's beauty: Architect Antoni Gaudí found his inspiration in the forms of nature. His distinctive architectural designs, such as the Sagrada Família in Barcelona, are a testament to the creative genius that can be drawn from the organic shapes and patterns found in the natural world. Gaudí's work seamlessly blends architecture with the beauty of nature, inviting us to explore the harmonious relationship between humanity and the environment.

Scientific exploration: The study of physics and quantum mechanics has sparked the creativity of many artists and writers. Authors like Douglas Adams, in his cult classic *The Hitchhiker's Guide to the Galaxy*, and artists like Salvador Dalí drew inspiration from the mind-bending concepts of science. Adams' witty and satirical take on the universe has become a beloved piece of science fiction literature.

Everyday life and routine: Renowned poet William Carlos Williams often found inspiration in the mundane aspects of daily life. His poem "The Red Wheelbarrow" celebrates the beauty in ordinary objects, reminding us that creativity can flourish in the simplicity of everyday moments. Williams' minimalist approach to poetry highlights the profound within the ordinary.

Historical examples of unconventional creativity:

- *Hedy Lamarr:* The glamorous Hollywood actress Hedy Lamarr was also an inventor. During World War II, she co-patented a frequency-hopping spread spectrum communication system that laid the groundwork for modern wireless technology, including Wi-Fi and Bluetooth. Lamarr's innovative thinking transcended the silver screen, leaving an enduring impact on our digital world.

- *Alexander Graham Bell:* Beyond inventing the telephone, Bell was deeply interested in sound and communication. He experimented with teaching speech to the deaf and even attempted to create a device to help people hear better by transmitting sound vibrations through the teeth and skull. Bell's curiosity and inventive spirit extended beyond telecommunication, leading him to explore innovative avenues in hearing technology.

- *Lewis Carroll:* Author of *Alice's Adventures in Wonderland*, Lewis Carroll was a mathematician who often incorporated his love for logic and wordplay into his whimsical stories. His creativity blended the worlds of literature and mathematics, resulting in a fantastical realm filled with riddles and absurdity. Carroll's imaginative storytelling continues to enchant readers of all ages.

- *Marcel Duchamp:* Duchamp was known for challenging traditional notions of art. His "readymades" were ordinary objects like a urinal or a bicycle wheel that he declared as art. His work pushed the boundaries of artistic creativity, inviting viewers to question the definition of art itself. Duchamp's provocative approach to art has sparked discussions on the nature of creativity and artistic expression.

These examples remind us that creativity is not limited to the expected or conventional sources. It can arise from dreams, mistakes, adversity, and even the quirks of everyday life. By embracing and exploring these unconventional sources, we can tap into reservoirs of creativity that lie within us, waiting to be unleashed.

Unusual sources of creativity (continued)

9. *War and innovation:* World War II sparked incredible innovation, including the development of radar, penicillin, and the jet engine. The urgency of wartime pushed scientists

and engineers to harness their creative potential to develop lifesaving technologies.

10. *Home kitchen creations:* Ruth Wakefield's inventive moment in her home kitchen led to the creation of the chocolate chip cookie. Her decision to add chopped chocolate to cookie dough transformed the world of baking, delighting taste buds for generations.

11. *Doodles and sketches:* Architect Frank Gehry often begins his designs with simple sketches and doodles. His iconic structures, like the Guggenheim Museum in Bilbao, Spain, reflect the organic and fluid shapes that originate from these creative sketches.

12. *Childhood experiences:* The beloved children's author Roald Dahl drew inspiration from his childhood experiences and vivid imagination. His classic tales, including *Charlie and the Chocolate Factory* and *Matilda*, transport readers to whimsical and sometimes darkly humorous worlds.

Closing the chapter with quotes

As we wrap up this exploration into the unexpected sources of creativity, let's draw inspiration from the wisdom of creative minds who have embraced the unconventional and allowed their creative sparks to shine:

> *Creativity is seeing what everyone else has seen and thinking what no one else has thought. (Albert Einstein)*

> *Imagination is more important than knowledge. For knowledge is limited, whereas imagination embraces the entire world, stimulating progress, giving birth to evolution. (Albert Einstein)*

Creativity takes courage. (Henri Matisse)

The worst enemy to creativity is self-doubt. (Sylvia Plath)

Creativity is intelligence having fun. (Albert Einstein)

I am seeking. I am striving. I am in it with all my heart. (Vincent van Gogh)

The painter tries to master color, the chef to master taste, and the musician to master sound. Only the writer does not strive for mastery over his medium, only his message. (Gabriel Garcia Marquez)

The most beautiful experience we can have is the mysterious. It is the fundamental emotion that stands at the cradle of true art and true science. (Albert Einstein)

May these quotes serve as a reminder that creativity knows no bounds, and its wellspring can be found in the most unexpected places. As you embark on your own creative journey, keep your senses open to the unconventional, for therein lies the magic of innovation and imagination with boundless creativity and unwavering curiosity.

4

The Power of Collaboration

In the heat of battle, a profound lesson emerges—one that transcends the battleground and extends its reach into the realm of human creativity. As a soldier in the United States Army, I learned the vital importance of unity and teamwork. Combat taught me that organized, coordinated effort is often the key to prevailing against chaos. But the truth is, the principle of collaboration isn't confined to warfare alone. It's a fundamental tenet that underpins human existence and creativity. It resonates in the harmonious symphonies of music, the strokes of an artist's brush, the grandeur of architectural marvels, and the leaps of innovation in technology.

Collaboration and creativity: Consider the iconic musical partnership of John Lennon and Paul McCartney. Their creative synergy produced timeless melodies and lyrics that resonate across generations. One's lyrical brilliance complemented the other's melodic genius, and together, they crafted songs that changed the world. In the realm of technology, Steve Jobs and Steve Wozniak formed a dynamic duo that revolutionized the digital age. Jobs, the visionary and marketer, found his counterpart in Wozniak, the engineering wizard. Their collaboration gave birth to Apple Inc., a company that transformed the way we live, work, and connect.

The creative cauldron: brainstorming: At the heart of collaboration lies the exchange of ideas—a crucible where creativity sparks and flourishes. This exchange isn't a haphazard toss of concepts into the wind but a structured process. It's a dance of thoughts and perspectives where each idea serves as a spark that fuels a collective flame. This structured approach, known as brainstorming, is where innovation is forged. It's a gathering where minds converge, ideas flow, and the mosaic of innovation takes shape. It's about listening, refining, and building upon each other's contributions until the brilliance of collective thinking emerges.

Collaborative ventures across fields: In the world of cinema, directors realize their visions through the collaborative efforts of actors, cinematographers, costume designers, and countless others. Each individual brings unique talents to the table, contributing to a tapestry of storytelling that captivates audiences. The world of art, too, is a testament to the power of collaboration. Artists inspire and challenge each other, pushing the boundaries of creativity and transcending conventions. In the sphere of technology, cross-disciplinary teams merge expertise from various fields to create groundbreaking inventions that reshape our world.

Crossing boundaries for innovation: Innovation thrives when boundaries are crossed. When individuals from different backgrounds unite, wielding their distinct skills and perspectives, magic happens. It's the physicist and the musician collaborating to create an immersive audiovisual experience. It's the biologist and the architect designing sustainable cities of the future. It's the poet and the scientist exploring the cosmos through the language of art.

The lesson of collaboration, learned in the crucible of battle, is universal. It transcends the battlefield and permeates every facet of human existence. It is a truth etched into the DNA of our species, a testament to the power of individuals working together toward a common goal.

Artistic alliances: In the realm of creativity, partnerships have often yielded spectacular results. Think of the timeless beauty captured in the works of Claude Monet and Pierre-Auguste Renoir during the Impressionist movement. These artists collaborated in the pursuit of capturing light, nature, and fleeting moments on canvas, forever altering the course of art history. Creative partnerships extend far beyond the world of painting.

Consider the poetic synergy of lyricist Bernie Taupin and musician Elton John. Their partnership resulted in an unparalleled catalog of songs that have become anthems of our lives.

Collaboration and innovation: In the world of innovation, the power of collaboration is equally evident. The story of Steve Jobs and Steve Wozniak is a shining example. Jobs, with his visionary ideas and marketing genius, needed the technical expertise of Wozniak to bring Apple's revolutionary products to life. Together, they ignited a technological revolution that endures to this day.

The art of brainstorming: Central to successful collaboration is the art of brainstorming. It's here that ideas collide, merge, and evolve into something greater than the sum of their parts. Brainstorming isn't just a random exchange of thoughts; it's a structured process of creativity. It's about creating an environment where ideas flow freely, where no suggestion is too outrageous and where the collective mind can transcend limits.

Harmonious creativity: Collaboration finds its most striking resonance in the world of music. Here, diverse talents merge seamlessly to produce harmonious symphonies and unforgettable melodies. The Beatles, one of the most iconic bands in history, exemplify this. Each member contributed a unique voice and perspective, resulting in a musical legacy that continues to inspire generations.

From chaos to innovation: In the crucible of combat, organization and teamwork ensure survival and success. Similarly, in the world of creativity, collaboration is the compass that guides us through the chaos of ideas, the maze of innovation, and the storm of artistic expression.

As we delve deeper into the heart of collaboration, we'll explore the partnerships, the brainstorming sessions, and the cross-disciplinary endeavors that have shaped our world. We'll learn from the creative giants who have harnessed the power of collaboration to bring forth art, innovation, and transformation. But just as important, we'll uncover the tools and techniques that can help you tap into this universal force in your own creative journey.

By the end of this chapter, you'll not only appreciate the profound impact of collaboration but also possess the knowledge to leverage it for your creative pursuits. So let us journey together into the world of collaboration, where the whole is indeed greater than the sum of its parts and where creativity blossoms like a magnificent symphony.

The lesson of collaboration, learned in the crucible of battle, is universal. It transcends the battlefield and permeates every facet of human existence. It is a truth etched into the DNA of our species, a testament to the power of individuals working together toward a common goal.

Exercise: Collaborative Vision Board: Let's put the power of collaboration into practice. Gather a group of friends, colleagues, or fellow creatives for a collaborative vision board session. A vision board is a visual representation of your goals and aspirations. Here's how to create a collaborative one:

1. ***Gather supplies:*** Collect magazines, newspapers, colored paper, scissors, glue sticks, and a large poster board or canvas for each participant.

2. ***Set a theme:*** Choose a theme for your vision board session. It could be related to your creative goals, personal aspirations, or a shared project.

3. ***Individual creativity:*** Start with a brief solo brainstorming session. Each participant should cut out images, words, or phrases from the magazines and newspapers that resonate with their personal vision related to the chosen theme.

4. ***Collaborative collage:*** After the individual brainstorming, bring everyone together. Each participant takes turns presenting their cutouts and explaining how they relate to the theme.

5. ***Assemble the board:*** Collaboratively arrange and glue the cutouts onto the poster board or canvas. Encourage participants to overlap and blend their ideas, creating a visual tapestry of shared creativity.

6. ***Reflect and discuss:*** Once the collaborative vision board is complete, take some time to reflect on the collective vision. Discuss how the different elements contribute to the overall theme and how collaboration enhanced the creative process.

Here are some questions for the Collaborative Vision Board exercise:

1. *Describe your experience working on the collaborative vision board with your group or partner(s). How did this collective creative process feel compared to individual vision boarding?*

2. *Reflect on the central theme or goals of your collaborative vision board. What was the inspiration behind this theme, and how did it resonate with each participant?*

3. *Explore the concept of visual storytelling within the vision board. How did each contributor's images and elements contribute to a cohesive narrative or vision for the future?*

4. *Consider the power of shared intention and visualization in the collaborative process. How did working together to create a collective vision impact your sense of purpose and motivation?*

5. *Share any challenges or differences in perspective that arose during the creation of the vision board. How were these challenges addressed, and did they lead to unexpected creative outcomes?*

6. *Reflect on the diverse perspectives and backgrounds of your group or partner(s). How did this diversity enrich the content and ideas represented in the vision board?*

7. *Describe any moments of synchronicity or alignment that occurred during the collaborative vision boarding process. Did you notice common themes or symbols that emerged organically?*

8. *Explore the tangible and intangible aspects of the vision board. What physical objects or images did you include, and how did they reflect the vision? Additionally, how did the process of creating the vision board impact your collective energy and enthusiasm?*

9. *Reflect on the act of visualizing and manifesting your shared vision. How does this exercise align with the concept of GodMode and tapping into your creative potential?*

10. *Consider the potential for future collaborations or projects that may stem from the shared vision developed in this exercise. How might this vision board serve as a guiding light for your collective creative endeavors?*

11. *Finally, contemplate the broader significance of collaborative vision boards in fostering connection, shared goals, and creative synergy. How can this exercise be applied to other areas of life or work to bring about positive change?*

These questions are designed to facilitate reflection on the Collaborative Vision Board exercise, highlighting the power of collective creativity, shared intention, and visual storytelling in manifesting a shared vision for the future.

This exercise not only fosters collaboration but also allows participants to visualize their collective aspirations and creative goals. It's a powerful way to tap into the collaborative spirit and unlock new creative possibilities.

Harmonious creativity

Diverse talents merge seamlessly to produce harmonious symphonies and unforgettable melodies. The Beatles, one of the most iconic bands in history, exemplify this. Each member contributed a unique voice and perspective, resulting in a musical legacy that continues to inspire generations. In the world of music, the power of collaboration has been an enduring source of inspiration. Consider the case of Wolfgang Amadeus Mozart and Lorenzo Da Ponte. Mozart, a musical prodigy, met Da Ponte, a talented librettist, and their collaboration gave birth to some of the most beloved operas in history. Mozart's genius found its perfect complement in Da Ponte's lyrical storytelling. Together, they crafted masterpieces like *The Marriage of Figaro*, *Don Giovanni*, and *Cosi fan tutte*. These operas are not merely musical compositions; they are collaborative symphonies of creativity, where Mozart's melodies intertwine with Da Ponte's words to create transcendent art. The world of technology offers a striking example of collaboration's transformative power. In the early twentieth century, Thomas Edison and Nikola Tesla were pioneers in the field of electricity. While Edison championed direct current (DC), Tesla advocated for alternating current (AC). Their differing approaches sparked a bitter rivalry. However, it was George Westinghouse, a visionary entrepreneur, who saw the potential for collaboration.

Westinghouse recognized that combining the best elements of both DC and AC could revolutionize electrical power generation and distribution. Through collaboration, Edison's and Tesla's innovations merged into a unified electrical system, powering the modern world. The result was not only a triumph of technology but also a testament to the idea that collaboration can turn competition into innovation.

In the art world, the collaboration between Salvador Dalí and Walt Disney was nothing short of visionary. These two creative giants from vastly different worlds, surrealism and animation, came together to create the short film *Destino*. The project began in 1946 but remained unfinished for decades. It wasn't until 2003 that it was completed. *Destino* seamlessly merges Dalí's surreal landscapes and dreamlike imagery with Disney's animation expertise.

The result is a visual masterpiece that transcends the boundaries of art forms and demonstrates the boundless possibilities of collaboration.

Reflecting on collaboration

These historical examples serve as beacons of inspiration, illuminating the profound impact of collaboration in various creative realms. Mozart and Da Ponte, Edison and Tesla, Dalí and Disney— all remind us that when diverse talents unite, the results can be nothing short of extraordinary.

As we explore the essence of collaboration in this chapter, remember that the power to create, innovate, and transform exists within each of us. The collaborative spirit that drove these historical giants can also fuel your creative endeavors. By embracing collaboration and harnessing the collective genius of those around you, you can unlock new realms of creativity and achieve feats that surpass your wildest dreams.

Further reading

If the alchemy of transformation has ignited your curiosity, there's a treasure trove of knowledge waiting to be explored. Dive deeper into the world of creativity, self-discovery, and transformation with these recommended resources:

1. *The Alchemist* by Paulo Coelho: A timeless novel that explores the journey of self-discovery and transformation.
2. *The Hero with a Thousand Faces* by Joseph Campbell: Delve into the hero's journey, a universal narrative pattern that underscores transformation and personal growth.
3. *Mindset: The New Psychology of Success* by Carol S. Dweck: Uncover the power of mindset in shaping your ability to adapt and transform.
4. *The Art of Possibility* by Rosamund Stone Zander and Benjamin Zander: Discover the transformative potential of reframing your perspective and embracing creativity.
5. *Creativity, Inc.* by Ed Catmull and Amy Wallace: A peek behind the scenes at Pixar Animation Studios, offering insights into fostering creativity and innovation.
6. *The Power of Habit* by Charles Duhigg: Explore the science behind habit formation and how it can influence personal transformation.

Quotes and insights

As we close the chapter on the alchemy of transformation, let these words from visionaries, artists, and thinkers resonate with you:

> **The only way to make sense out of change is to plunge into it, move with it, and join the dance. (Alan Watts)**

> **Your task is not to seek for love, but merely to seek and find all the barriers within yourself that you have built against it. (Rumi)**

The journey of a thousand miles begins with one step. (Lao Tzu)

Creativity is intelligence having fun. (Albert Einstein)

The caterpillar does all the work, but the butterfly gets all the publicity. (George Carlin)

May these words and resources be your guiding lights as you embark on your own transformative journey. Remember, within you lies the power to transmute the ordinary into the extraordinary and to become the alchemist of your own destiny.

Closing thoughts

In the chapters that follow, we'll delve even deeper into the art and science of collaboration. We'll uncover practical techniques and strategies to enhance your collaborative efforts, whether in music, technology, art, or any creative pursuit. By the end, you'll not only appreciate the profound impact of collaboration but also possess the tools to harness this universal force for your own creative genius. So let us continue our exploration, inspired by the collaborative triumphs of history, as we unlock the true power of creativity through the art of collaboration.

5

Creativity as a Continuum

In the early nineteenth century, Ada Lovelace—an English mathematician and writer—collaborated with Charles Babbage, a pioneer in mechanical computing. Their partnership gave birth to the analytical engine, an early precursor to the modern computer. While Babbage designed the hardware, it was Ada Lovelace who envisioned the machine's potential beyond number crunching. She recognized that it could be programmed to perform any task, not just calculations.

Ada Lovelace's innovative thinking led her to write what is now considered the world's first computer program. Her notes on Babbage's work included an algorithm for the analytical engine to calculate Bernoulli numbers, a pioneering concept in computer programming. Her visionary ideas laid the foundation for the digital age, showcasing the power of interdisciplinary thinking in the realm of technology.

During the Italian Renaissance, the city of Florence became a hotbed of creativity and innovation. Artists, scientists, and thinkers from various disciplines converged in workshops and salons, sparking cross-disciplinary collaborations that reshaped the course of history. One remarkable example is the partnership between Leonardo da Vinci and the anatomist Marcantonio della Torre. Their collaboration involved da Vinci's meticulous anatomical drawings and della Torre's groundbreaking anatomical research. This interdisciplinary synergy led to a deeper understanding of the human body with da

Vinci's anatomical sketches demonstrating a level of precision and insight far ahead of his time.

Demystifying creativity

Creativity, often shrouded in myths and misconceptions, is not the exclusive domain of artists, writers, or musicians. It is not an elusive gift granted to a chosen few at birth. Creativity is a dynamic and accessible force that resides within each of us. It's a spectrum of possibilities waiting to be explored.

Consider this: every time you solve a problem, adapt to a new situation, or make a decision, you are exercising your creative muscles. Creativity extends beyond traditional artistic endeavors. It's present in your daily life, in the choices you make, and in your ability to navigate an ever-changing world. Think about the chef who experiments with ingredients to create a new recipe, the teacher who designs engaging lessons to inspire students, or the entrepreneur who devises innovative solutions to pressing challenges. These are all examples of everyday creativity where individuals harness their creative potential to excel in their chosen fields.

Creativity across fields: Creativity knows no boundaries. It transcends disciplines and permeates every aspect of human endeavor. From the laboratory of a scientist to the boardroom of a business executive, creativity is a driving force behind innovation and progress. Consider the groundbreaking work of Marie Curie, the physicist and chemist who made pioneering discoveries in the field of radioactivity. Her relentless curiosity and innovative experiments not only earned her Nobel Prizes in both physics and chemistry but also revolutionized our understanding of the fundamental building blocks of matter.

Fostering a creative mindset: Unlocking your creative potential begins with cultivating a creative mindset. It's about approaching challenges with an open heart and an inquisitive spirit. It's the willingness to embrace ambiguity and learn from failures. A creative mindset values curiosity, resilience, and adaptability. Practical techniques can help you nurture this mindset. Daily practices of journaling, brainstorming, or simply observing the world around you can spark new ideas and perspectives. Meditation and mindfulness can sharpen your focus and connect you with your inner wellspring of creativity.

The power of interdisciplinary thinking: Creativity thrives at the intersection of disciplines. Often, it's the synthesis of insights from multiple fields that leads to breakthroughs. Consider the genius of Leonardo da Vinci, who seamlessly merged art and science. His notebooks are a testament to his interdisciplinary thinking, where sketches of inventions coexist with studies of anatomy and art. Interdisciplinary thinking encourages you to explore connections between seemingly unrelated ideas, fostering innovation and fresh perspectives. It's about breaking down the silos that can limit creativity and embracing the diversity of thought.

Creative collaborations: Collaboration, a force explored in earlier chapters, continues to play a pivotal role in expanding creativity. When individuals with diverse backgrounds and expertise come together, magic happens. The collision of ideas and perspectives often leads to solutions that transcend the capabilities of any single mind. Think of the Apollo program, which brought together engineers, scientists, and astronauts from different disciplines to achieve the historic moon landing. It was a testament to the power of collaboration in pushing the boundaries of human achievement.

Exercises and reflections: In this chapter, as in previous ones, you'll find exercises and reflections designed to help you embrace creativity as a continuum in your life. These exercises will encourage you to recognize your own everyday creative moments, explore interdisciplinary connections, and foster a creative mindset. Creativity is not a finite resource. It's an infinite wellspring within you. By understanding that creativity is a continuum, you'll unlock new possibilities and realize that the creative spark is always within reach, waiting for you to ignite it.

Creativity, often shrouded in myths and misconceptions, is not the exclusive domain of artists, writers, or musicians. It is not an elusive gift granted to a chosen few at birth. Creativity is a dynamic and accessible force that resides within each of us. It's a spectrum of possibilities waiting to be explored.

Everyday creativity: My own journey into the realm of creativity was shaped profoundly by my mother, a resourceful and imaginative woman. She had a unique talent for turning thrift store treasures into dazzling home decor, transforming humble finds into objects of beauty. Her secret was not just her artistic eye but her unwavering belief that there's always more than one way to complete a project. She instilled in me the value of thinking outside the box, of approaching challenges with a sense of possibility and resourcefulness.

Unlocking your creative potential begins with cultivating a creative mindset. It's about approaching challenges with an open heart and an inquisitive spirit. It's the willingness to embrace ambiguity and learn from failures. A creative mindset values curiosity, resilience, and adaptability.

Exercise: The Daily Creativity Journal: To nurture your creative mindset, start a "Daily Creativity Journal." Each day, jot down at least one moment where you applied creativity, no matter how small. It could be solving a household problem, coming up with a clever work solution, or even finding a unique way to express yourself. Over time, you'll develop a deeper appreciation for the everyday creativity that surrounds you. The power of interdisciplinary thinking creativity thrives at the intersection of disciplines.

Often, it's the synthesis of insights from multiple fields that leads to breakthroughs. Consider the genius of Leonardo da Vinci, who seamlessly merged art and science. His notebooks are a testament to his interdisciplinary thinking, where sketches of inventions coexist with studies of anatomy and art.

Exercise 2: The Cross-Pollination Challenge: To embrace interdisciplinary thinking, challenge yourself to explore connections between two seemingly unrelated fields. Pick a topic from your area of interest or expertise and another from a completely different domain. How do they intersect? What novel ideas emerge when you bring their principles together? This exercise can lead to surprising insights and innovative solutions.

Instructions: Select two unrelated concepts: Choose two concepts, topics, or fields that are seemingly unrelated to each other. For example, you could select music and botany. *Brainstorm connections:* Spend some time brainstorming how these two concepts might intersect or share common elements. What do they have in common no matter how obscure or symbolic it may seem? Consider historical references, metaphors, or even shared emotions.

Create analogies: Craft analogies or metaphors that link the two concepts. Think about how elements from one concept can shed light on the other. For instance, how might the growth patterns of plants relate to the composition of a musical masterpiece?

Artistic expression: Express your newfound connections artistically. You can create a piece of art, write a poem, compose a short story, or even design a visual representation that captures the essence of this cross-pollination.

Reflect and share: Take a moment to reflect on the process and what you've created. What insights or revelations have emerged from this exercise? How might these connections be applied to your own creative journey?

Example: Let's say you've chosen architecture and culinary arts. You might discover that the precision and attention to detail in both fields are paramount. The layout of a building can be likened to the structure of a well-crafted dish. The way ingredients are layered and presented in a meal could mirror the arrangement of architectural elements. With these connections in mind, you could create a visual representation that fuses the two or write a short story where a chef's culinary creations are inspired by iconic architectural designs. Remember, the power of cross-pollination lies in its ability to spark fresh ideas and perspectives. Embrace the unexpected connections and let them fuel your creative journey in ways you never imagined.

Historical example 1: The Wright Brothers

Consider the collaboration of the Wright brothers, Wilbur and Orville, who dared to defy gravity and conquer the skies. Their innovative thinking and tireless experimentation revolutionized aviation. They combined engineering know-how with a deep understanding of aerodynamics to create the first powered, controlled, and sustained flight in 1903. Their collaboration not only changed the course of history but also opened up new realms of exploration.

Historical example 2: The enlightenment salons

In eighteenth-century Europe, the enlightenment salons served as vibrant hubs of intellectual exchange and creative collaboration. Hosted by influential women like Madame Geoffrin and Madame de Stael, these gatherings brought together thinkers, writers, scientists, and artists from various disciplines. It was within the spirited discussions and shared ideas of these salons that many enlightenment-era ideals were born, shaping the course of philosophy, science, and culture.

Beyond its practical applications, creativity also carries profound spiritual implications. It is a means of connecting with the divine, a way of tapping into the boundless source of inspiration that exists in the universe. When we create, we participate in the act of bringing something new into existence, mirroring the creative force of the cosmos itself. Think of the act of meditation, where we quiet the mind and open ourselves to insights and ideas that seem to flow from a higher source. In these moments, we glimpse the vast reservoir of creativity that resides within us as if we are channels for a greater creative energy. This realization hints at a profound truth: that we are not mere spectators in the universe's creative process; we are active participants, cocreators with the divine.

Exercise: The creative reflection

To conclude this chapter and prepare yourself for the creative journey ahead, I invite you to engage in a Creative Reflection exercise.

1. **Find a quiet and comfortable space where you won't be disturbed.**

2. **Close your eyes and take a few deep, cleansing breaths. Inhale deeply, hold for a moment, and exhale slowly. Allow any tension or stress to melt away.**

3. **With your eyes closed, visualize a serene, boundless ocean of creativity stretching to the horizon. Imagine its shimmering waters reflecting the endless possibilities of your creative potential.**

4. **As you gaze upon this metaphorical ocean, consider the unique ways in which creativity has manifested in your life. Reflect on moments when you've solved problems,**

found innovative solutions, or expressed yourself in a way that felt truly original.

5.   *Think about the people, experiences, and circumstances that have influenced your creative journey. Recognize the interconnectedness of your creativity with the world around you.*

6.   *Now imagine yourself stepping into this ocean of creativity, submerging yourself in its waters. Feel the fluidity and boundless nature of your creative energy. Allow it to flow through you, renewing your sense of purpose and inspiration.*

7.   *As you immerse yourself in this creative ocean, set an intention for your creative path ahead. What do you aspire to create? How do you wish to harness your creativity to make a positive impact on your life and the world?*

8. *When you're ready, slowly open your eyes, carrying with you the revitalized awareness of your creative potential.*

In this chapter, we've explored creativity as a continuum that extends beyond traditional artistic domains. Creativity is not an exclusive gift; it's a force inherent in each of us. We've learned that everyday creativity shapes our lives, from solving problems to making decisions. Interdisciplinary thinking, exemplified by historical figures like Ada Lovelace and the Renaissance polymaths, reveals how creativity flourishes at the intersection of different fields.

We've practiced nurturing a creative mindset and embracing the limitless nature of creativity. Moreover, we've delved into the spiritual dimensions of creativity, recognizing that it connects us to a higher source of inspiration, making us cocreators with the divine. This understanding invites us to tap into boundless reservoirs of creative energy within ourselves. As we move forward, remember that creativity is not confined to specific activities—it's a way of living. By recognizing the creative potential in every moment and embracing a multidisciplinary perspective, you'll discover that creativity is a journey without boundaries.

Allow these insights to guide your creative endeavors. As you explore the vast spectrum of creativity, remember that you are not separate from the universe's creative process; you are an integral part of it. The exercises and reflections in this chapter are tools to help you unlock your creative potential. In the chapters ahead, we'll delve even deeper into practical strategies for nurturing creativity in your life.

By the end of our journey, you'll not only understand that creativity knows no bounds but also possess the tools to infuse creativity into every facet of your existence. Let us continue this voyage together, where creativity knows no limits and where your creative potential is boundless.

Inspirational quotes

Creativity is intelligence having fun. (Albert Einstein)

The painter tries to master color while the musician is an expert in time. (Leonardo da Vinci)

The greatest scientists are always artists as well. (Albert Einstein)

Creativity is the greatest rebellion in existence. (Osho)

You are the universe experiencing itself. (Alan Watts)

6

The Creative Process Unveiled

Creativity is often perceived as an enigmatic process, a mysterious wellspring from which ideas emerge seemingly out of nowhere. In this chapter, we will unveil the inner workings of the creative process, demystifying it and providing you with practical insights to harness its power.

The four stages of creativity

The creative process can be distilled into four distinct stages: preparation, incubation, illumination, and verification. These stages are not linear; they intertwine and overlap, reflecting the complex nature of creativity.

1. *Preparation:* This is the phase where you gather information, immerse yourself in the subject matter, and define the problem or challenge. We'll explore techniques for effective preparation, including research, brainstorming, and goal setting. This stage involves immersing yourself in the subject matter, gathering knowledge, and exploring diverse perspectives. It's akin to tilling the soil, preparing it for the seeds of inspiration to take root. During this phase, you accumulate information, insights, and experiences that will

serve as the raw materials for your creative endeavor. It's the research, the reading, the brainstorming, and the endless curiosity that lay the foundation for what's to come.

2. *Incubation:* Once the seeds are sown, they need time to germinate. Incubation is the stage of waiting and allowing the subconscious mind to work its magic. It's the aha moment that strikes when you least expect it—while you're in the shower, taking a walk, or daydreaming in a café. This phase is marked by a sense of detachment from the problem or project at hand. It's where ideas simmer beneath the surface, mingling and cross-pollinating until they mature into fully formed concepts.

3. *Illumination:* When the time is right, illumination dawns. This is the moment of revelation, when a brilliant idea bursts forth from the depths of your mind. It's the eureka moment that every creator cherishes. During illumination, disparate elements suddenly connect, and you see a solution, a story, a melody, or a vision with crystal clarity. It's the creative spark that propels you forward, igniting your passion and setting your project in motion.

4. *Verification:* The final stage involves refining and testing your creative idea or solution. We'll discuss techniques for validation, experimentation, and feedback. Creativity is not without its challenges. We'll examine common creative blocks and provide strategies to overcome them. Whether you're facing self-doubt, fear of failure, or a lack of inspiration, these techniques will help you navigate the creative process with confidence.

Creativity is a skill that can be honed and developed. We'll explore practices and habits that foster creativity, from mindfulness and meditation to embracing failure as a stepping stone to success. By the end of this chapter, you'll have a deep understanding of how creativity operates and practical tools to enhance your creative endeavors. Creative blocks and how to overcome them is not without its challenges.

We'll examine common creative blocks and provide strategies to overcome them. Whether you're facing self-doubt, fear of failure, or a lack of inspiration, these techniques will help you navigate the creative process with confidence. Cultivating creativity and flow creativity flourishes when you're aligned with your desires and in a state of flow.

This chapter emphasizes the importance of enjoying your creative projects and listening to your inner desires. If you find yourself running out of creative energy for one project, switch to another that ignites your passion. The key is to be in tune with your inner creative compass.

Exercise: The Creative Energy Gauge: To gauge your creative energy and alignment with your desires, create a simple chart with your ongoing creative projects. Rate each project on a scale of one to ten based on how enjoyable and exciting it currently feels. Take note of projects that score low and consider why. Are they aligned with your passions and interests? Use this exercise to realign your creative focus with what truly ignites your enthusiasm.

Exercise 2: The Creative Flow Map: Imagine your creative process as a river and your projects as various streams branching from it. Create a visual representation of this flow map. Identify the projects that naturally flow from your creative source. Which projects make you lose track of time and immerse you in a state of flow? These are the projects that resonate with your inner desires and fuel your creativity. By the end of this chapter, you'll not only understand the mechanics of the creative process but also possess practical tools to enhance your creative endeavors.

Isabella Bird: The intrepid Victorian explorer and travel writer

Isabella Bird, born in 1831, was an intrepid Victorian explorer and travel writer whose remarkable journeys across the globe ignited her creativity and left an indelible mark on the world of exploration and literature. Her life and adventures serve as a testament to the profound connection between exploration and artistic expression.

Isabella Bird's early life was marked by frailty and health issues. Suffering from a spinal ailment, she sought refuge in travel as a form of therapy and escape from her physical limitations. Her first significant journey took her to North America in 1854, where she explored the expansive territories of Canada and the United States.

What set Isabella Bird apart from her contemporaries was her unconventional approach to travel. She often ventured into remote and challenging regions, far removed from the comforts of Victorian society. Notably, she explored the Rocky Mountains, Hawaiian Islands, and Australia, documenting her experiences through her vivid and captivating writing.

Isabella Bird's written accounts of her travels became her creative outlet, and her books quickly gained popularity. Her prose was both poetic and insightful, providing readers with a window into the diverse cultures and landscapes she encountered. Among her most renowned works is *The Hawaiian Archipelago: Six Months among the Palm Groves, Coral Reefs, and Volcanoes of the Sandwich Islands*, which remains a classic in travel literature.

Isabella Bird's creative spirit flourished amidst the breathtaking landscapes and diverse cultures she encountered during her travels. Her writings were infused with a deep appreciation for the beauty of the natural world and the resilience of the human spirit. She demonstrated how exploration could be a wellspring of artistic inspiration as her prose vividly captured the essence of the places she visited.

Isabella Bird's fearless exploration of the unknown paved the way for future generations of female travelers and writers. She challenged societal norms and gender expectations, proving that women could be intrepid explorers and gifted storytellers. Her legacy endures not only in her writings but also in the inspiration she continues to provide to adventurers and creatives alike. Isabella Bird's life story underscores the profound connection between exploration and artistic expression. Her journey from a fragile young woman to a trailblazing explorer and writer serves as a compelling example of how venturing into the unknown can kindle the flames of creativity, leaving an enduring mark on the world.

Josephine Baker: The legendary dancer,
singer, and civil rights activist

Josephine Baker—born in 1906 in St. Louis, Missouri—was a legendary dancer, singer, and civil rights activist whose life exemplified the extraordinary power of creativity in breaking down barriers and effecting profound social change. Her journey from humble beginnings to international stardom is a testament to the transformative potential of art as a force for justice and equality.

Josephine's early life was marked by hardship and adversity. She grew up in a racially segregated America, facing discrimination and limited opportunities. At the age of nineteen, she embarked on a journey to France, seeking escape from the racial prejudice she experienced in the United States.

In Paris, Josephine found a place where her talent and creativity could flourish without the constraints of racial discrimination. Her performances as a dancer, characterized by her uninhibited energy and charisma, captivated audiences across Europe. She soon became a sensation at the Folies Bergère and other renowned venues.

Josephine's creative expression went beyond the confines of entertainment. She used her fame and artistry as a platform for activism. During World War II, she worked as a spy for the French Resistance, smuggling important information hidden in her sheet music and clothing. Her dedication to the fight against fascism earned her the Croix de Guerre, France's highest military honor.

Josephine Baker's commitment to civil rights was unwavering. She refused to perform for segregated audiences in the United States, and she spoke out against racial injustice both in her homeland and abroad. Her return to the United States in the 1950s was marked by a refusal to accept segregation, even in the face of threats and violence.

Beyond her activism, Josephine Baker was a passionate humanitarian. She adopted twelve children from diverse backgrounds, forming what she called her "Rainbow Tribe." Her commitment to promoting racial harmony and understanding through her family exemplified her belief in the power of love and art to transcend prejudice.

Josephine Baker's legacy endures as a symbol of courage, creativity, and advocacy for civil rights. She demonstrated how art could be a powerful tool for social change, breaking racial barriers and challenging injustice. Her impact on both the entertainment industry and the Civil Rights Movement remains profound.

Josephine Baker's life story serves as a powerful reminder that creativity can be a force not only for personal expression but also for societal transformation. Her unwavering commitment to justice and equality through the medium of art continues to inspire generations of artists and activists around the world.

Roald Dahl: The beloved author of whimsical tales

Roald Dahl—born in 1916 in Llandaff, Wales—remains a beloved author of children's books whose whimsical tales continue to captivate young readers and adults alike. His literary contributions not only showcase the timeless appeal of storytelling but also emphasize the transformative power of imagination and creativity.

Roald Dahl's early life was marked by adventure and challenges. He attended various schools, and his experiences there inspired his later works, which often depicted the whimsical and sometimes dark aspects of childhood. His fascination with storytelling and literature was kindled during his formative years. Dahl's life took a dramatic turn during World War II when he joined the Royal Air Force as a fighter pilot.

After surviving a plane crash in Libya, he was stationed in Nairobi, Kenya, where he began his writing career. His stories, inspired by his experiences in Africa, were published in magazines, marking the beginning of his literary journey.

Roald Dahl's most enduring legacy lies in his children's books, which are characterized by their whimsical and imaginative narratives. Classics like *Charlie and the Chocolate Factory*, *Matilda*, *James and the Giant Peach*, and *The BFG* have captured the hearts of generations of young readers. His ability to create fantastical worlds and endearing characters showcases the enduring appeal of storytelling as a vehicle for nurturing creativity and inspiring wonder.

Dahl's stories often revolve around the triumph of the imagination and creativity over adversity. Whether it's a young boy winning a golden ticket to a magical chocolate factory or a precocious girl developing telekinetic powers, his narratives encourage readers to embrace their unique abilities and view the world with a sense of wonder.

In addition to his children's literature, Dahl's works for adults often featured dark humor and unexpected twists. His short stories for grown-ups, collected in books like *Tales of the Unexpected*, showcased his talent for crafting suspenseful narratives with unexpected endings. This versatility as a writer further underscores his creative prowess.

Roald Dahl's stories continue to be cherished by readers of all ages. His books have been translated into numerous languages and adapted into films, stage productions, and even theme park attractions. His enduring impact on literature and the world of storytelling is a testament to the lasting power of creativity to inspire, entertain, and provoke thought.

Roald Dahl's legacy as a beloved author demonstrates how storytelling can serve as a conduit for creativity, imagination, and the exploration of the human experience. His enchanting tales encourage readers to embrace their inner storytellers and find joy in the limitless possibilities of the written word. This expanded biography of Roald Dahl covers his early life, adventures in Africa, contributions to children's literature, emphasis on imagination and creativity, forays into adult literature, and his enduring impact as a beloved author.

Jean-Michel Basquiat: The trailblazing
artist who redefined creativity

Jean-Michel Basquiat—born in 1960 in Brooklyn, New York—was a trailblazing artist who transcended artistic conventions and challenged the boundaries of creativity. From his early days as a graffiti artist to his transformation into a celebrated painter, Basquiat's life and work exemplify the boundless and unconventional nature of artistic expression. Basquiat's journey into the world of art began with graffiti. As a teenager, he roamed the streets of New York City, using the pseudonym "SAMO" to create thought-provoking and enigmatic graffiti works. His unique blend of words, symbols, and social commentary quickly garnered attention, making him a notable figure in the burgeoning street art scene of the late 1970s and early 1980s.

Basquiat's transition from graffiti to fine art was both meteoric and unconventional. His raw, expressive style caught the eye of the art world, and he rapidly gained recognition as a painter. His works often featured a fusion of text and imagery, reflecting the influence of his graffiti roots and his fascination with language, identity, and culture. What set Basquiat apart was his unapologetic approach to challenging artistic conventions. His paintings defied traditional boundaries and categories, blending elements of abstraction, figuration, and symbolism. He delved into themes of race, power, history, and the human condition, creating works that were simultaneously deeply personal and universally resonant.

Basquiat's collaborations with other artists, including Andy Warhol, further demonstrated his willingness to explore new creative avenues. His partnership with Warhol resulted in a series of collaborative artworks that bridged the gap between street art and the mainstream art world. Jean-Michel Basquiat's impact on contemporary art cannot be overstated.

He opened doors for artists to embrace the unconventional and the unorthodox. His ability to merge high and low art, confront social issues, and communicate profound ideas through his work paved the way for a new generation of artists who refuse to be confined by artistic boundaries. Basquiat's life and career are a testament to the idea that creativity knows no bounds.

He proved that art can emerge from the streets and that unconventional methods and unconventional artists have a valuable place in the world of creativity. His legacy continues to inspire artists to break free from conventions and express themselves authentically. Jean-Michel Basquiat's story serves as a powerful reminder that creativity is not limited by tradition or expectation. His fearless exploration of the uncharted territories of artistic expression challenges us all to embrace our own unique creative voices and redefine what is possible within the realm of creativity.

Temple Grandin: A pioneer in science and autism advocacy

Temple Grandin—born in 1947 in Boston, Massachusetts—is a pioneering scientist and autism advocate, who harnessed her unique perspective to revolutionize both the fields of animal science and autism awareness. Her remarkable journey underscores the creative potential within diverse minds and serves as a testament to the power of resilience, innovation, and empathy.

From an early age, Temple Grandin faced significant challenges related to autism. In a time when understanding of the condition was limited, she struggled with social interactions and sensory sensitivities. Despite these obstacles, Grandin's innate curiosity and determination shone through.

One of Grandin's most notable contributions has been in the field of animal science. Her deep empathy for animals led her to develop innovative and humane livestock handling systems. Through her unique perspective and insights, she designed cattle chutes and corrals that reduced stress and improved the welfare of animals in the meat industry.

Her work revolutionized the way animals are treated in the agricultural sector and continues to be widely adopted. Temple Grandin's personal experience with autism propelled her into the role of a passionate advocate for individuals on the autism spectrum.

She recognized that autism brought with it unique strengths and ways of thinking that could be harnessed for creative and productive purposes.

Through her speaking engagements and writing, she raised awareness about autism and championed the idea that neurodiversity is an asset to society. Grandin's ability to see the world through a different lens, both in her work with animals and her advocacy for those with autism, exemplifies the creative potential that lies within diverse minds.

She demonstrated that embracing and nurturing individual perspectives, rather than trying to conform to a perceived norm, can lead to breakthrough innovations and positive change. Temple Grandin's contributions have earned her numerous accolades and honors. She has been recognized as one of *Time* magazine's "100 Most Influential People" and received the Presidential Medal of Freedom. Her impact on animal welfare and autism advocacy is immeasurable, and her story continues to inspire countless individuals worldwide.

Temple Grandin's life and work illustrate the profound impact that creativity, empathy, and resilience can have on society. Her ability to harness her unique perspective to drive positive change in multiple fields is a testament to the limitless creative potential within all individuals regardless of their neurodiversity. Temple Grandin's legacy serves as a reminder that diversity of thought and experience is a wellspring of creativity and innovation. Her unwavering commitment to improving the lives of animals and individuals with autism has left an indelible mark on both fields and continues to inspire generations to embrace their own unique creative perspectives.

Exercise: The Creative Perspective Journal: In honor of Temple Grandin's remarkable ability to harness her unique perspective, embark on a personal journey of self-discovery and creativity. Create a "Creative Perspective Journal" in which you document your daily observations, insights, and experiences from a unique point of view. Challenge yourself to view the world through a different lens, whether it's by focusing on small details others might overlook or by exploring a new perspective on familiar situations. Use this journal as a canvas for your creativity and let it become a valuable tool for self-expression and innovation.

   Instructions: *Select a journal:* Find a notebook or create a digital document dedicated to your Creative Perspective Journal.
   Daily reflections: Commit to making daily entries, even if they are brief. Reflect on your experiences, thoughts, and observations throughout the day. Consider moments of inspiration, challenges, or encounters that sparked your creativity.
   Ask questions: Pose questions to yourself about the world around you. These questions can be as specific or as open-ended as you like. For example, you might ask, "What if gravity worked in reverse?" or "How does light affect the way we perceive color?"
   Capture details: Pay attention to the details. Describe sights, sounds, textures, and emotions. Be vivid and specific in your descriptions as though you're painting a picture with words.
   Make connections: Draw connections between seemingly unrelated things. If you see a connection between a street performer's dance and the flow of a river, write it down. These connections are the raw material for your creative ideas.
   Experiment with perspectives: Challenge yourself to adopt different perspectives. Write from the viewpoint of an ant, a cloud, or a historical figure. This exercise helps you see the world through fresh eyes.
   Reflect and expand: At the end of each week, review your entries. Identify recurring themes, questions, or perspectives that resonate with you. Use these insights to guide your creative projects.
   Expand on ideas: When you discover an idea or perspective that intrigues you, expand on it. Write a short story, create a sketch, compose a poem, or brainstorm how it might influence a future project.
   Example: Imagine you notice the interplay of shadows and light while taking a walk in the park. You record your observations in your Creative Perspective Journal, describing the dance of leaves' shadows on the ground. Over time, you begin to experiment with incorporating this play of shadows and light into your artwork, pho-

tography, or storytelling, adding depth and emotion to your creations. Your Creative Perspective Journal becomes a treasure trove of unique viewpoints, ideas, and creative sparks that you can draw from whenever you need inspiration. Remember, your perspective is your superpower as a creator. It's what sets you apart and infuses your work with a distinctive flavor. By nurturing and refining your perspective through this journal, you'll unlock new dimensions of your creative potential.

Summary: The creative tapestry

In this chapter, we embarked on a journey through the lives and creative contributions of five remarkable individuals from diverse fields. Each of these creative explorers showcased the boundless nature of creativity and the power it wields to transcend conventions, shatter boundaries, and ignite change.

1. *Isabella Bird* demonstrated that exploration is not only a physical journey but a catalyst for artistic expression. Her intrepid travels fueled her creativity, illustrating how venturing into the unknown can kindle the flames of imagination.
2. *Josephine Baker*—a trailblazing dancer, singer, and civil rights activist—used her creativity to break down racial barriers and challenge injustice. Her story exemplifies how art can be a powerful tool for societal change.
3. *Roald Dahl*, the beloved author of whimsical tales, revealed the timeless appeal of storytelling. His ability to create fantastical worlds and endearing characters showcased the enduring power of imaginative narrative.
4. *Jean-Michel Basquiat*, a graffiti artist turned painter, defied artistic conventions and demonstrated that creativity knows no bounds. His bold and unconventional works challenged artistic norms and inspired others to think outside the box.

5. *Temple Grandin*, a pioneering scientist and autism advocate, harnessed her unique perspective to revolutionize animal science and autism awareness. Her life showcases the creative potential within diverse minds and emphasizes the importance of embracing individual perspectives.

Notable quotes

> *Embrace your uniqueness; it is your gift to the world. (Temple Grandin)*

> *The world needs all kinds of minds. (Temple Grandin)*

> *Creativity is intelligence having fun. (Albert Einstein)*

> *Imagination is more important than knowledge. (Albert Einstein)*

> *The only limit to our realization of tomorrow will be our doubts of today. (Franklin D. Roosevelt)*

As we conclude this chapter, let us reflect on the stories of these creative explorers and the wisdom they've left behind. Their journeys have illuminated the multifaceted nature of creativity, reminding us that it knows no boundaries and can be a catalyst for transformation and innovation in our own lives.

7

The Power of Focus

The extraordinary superpower of focus—a divine ability that enables us to channel our energy and drive toward our goals. For young individuals facing the myriad distractions of life, especially in challenging circumstances, focus becomes a beacon of hope and progress.

Growing up in Jacksonville, Florida, presented countless distractions and temptations. Those who chose paths filled with crime and trouble often paid a heavy price. Even being in the wrong place at the wrong time could cost you. The odds were stacked against many young lives, but the choice to resist those temptations was pivotal. We'll explore the importance of recognizing the forks in our life's road and choosing the path of focus and discipline.

Joining the air force just before the fateful events of 9/11 brought its own set of challenges and distractions. The discipline instilled by military life proved to be a guiding light for me. While I know people who faced the consequences of unfocused decisions, the journey of focus had begun, paving the way for personal and creative growth. The distractions and opportunities that Europe offered during my time stationed at Ramstein Air Base in Germany were abundant. Yet the lessons from my past experiences and the understanding that life could offer everything one desires but requires unwavering focus resonated deeply.

In our fast-paced, hyper-connected world, maintaining focus has become increasingly challenging. The constant barrage of notifications, the allure of social media, and the ever-present smartphone in our pockets all contribute to a continuous stream of distractions. This unprecedented level of digital stimuli has made it more difficult for individuals to concentrate on tasks, goals, and creative pursuits. As we navigate this digital landscape, it's important to recognize that our ability to focus is not only a personal asset but also a valuable skill that can significantly impact our lives. The paradox lies in the fact that while technology offers us incredible opportunities for creativity and productivity, it also presents the greatest hurdles to maintaining our focus.

Military examples of focus in decisive moments: The military provides numerous real-life examples of how focus plays a pivotal role in critical and decisive moments. Here are a few military scenarios where unwavering focus made a difference:

1. *The Battle of Stalingrad (World War II):* During this brutal and protracted battle, both Soviet and German soldiers had to maintain intense focus amidst relentless combat. Each decision, each moment of concentration, could mean the difference between life and death. The ability to stay focused on objectives, tactics, and survival was paramount.

2. *Special operations missions:* In elite military units like the navy SEALs or special forces, focus is a fundamental skill. These operators undergo rigorous training to hone their ability to concentrate in high-stress situations. Whether conducting a covert mission or facing unexpected challenges, maintaining focus is essential to success.

3. *Pilot training and combat:* Fighter pilots require an exceptional level of focus. They must process vast amounts of information in the cockpit, make split-second decisions, and stay calm under extreme pressure. The consequences of losing focus during aerial combat can be catastrophic.

4. *Sniper operations:* Snipers must remain incredibly focused for extended periods, often in remote and hostile environments. Their ability to stay patient and concentrated while

waiting for the right shot is a testament to the power of focus.

These military examples highlight the critical role of focus in high-stakes situations. In each case, individuals must filter out distractions, maintain mental clarity, and execute their missions with precision. Their training and discipline enable them to stay on target, even when faced with chaos and adversity. In our modern world, where distractions are abundant and attention spans are challenged, we can draw inspiration from these military examples. While our daily challenges may differ from those on the battlefield, the ability to harness the power of focus remains a timeless and invaluable skill. By acknowledging the difficulties we face in maintaining focus today and learning from those who have mastered it in extreme conditions, we can take steps to reclaim our own powers of concentration and apply them to our creative pursuits and personal growth.

We'll discuss how life sometimes grants us our desires, but it's our responsibility to stay focused on our goals.

Exercise: The Focus Decision Journal: Reflect on pivotal moments in their lives where they faced distractions and had to make choices. Prompt them to write about the decisions they made, the challenges they faced, and how focus played a role in shaping their path.

1. *Can you recall a specific moment in your life when you faced significant distractions or temptations that could have led you down a different path? Describe the circumstances.*

2. *What were the choices you had to make during that crucial moment? What factors influenced your decisions?*

3. *Reflect on the consequences that your choices had on your life's direction. How did your decisions impact your personal growth and creative journey?*

4. *Were there individuals, mentors, or role models who played a role in helping you stay focused and make the right choices? How did they influence your path?*

5. *In hindsight, do you believe that your ability to focus played a significant role in your ability to resist distractions and stay on course? Explain.*

6. *How has your understanding of focus evolved over the years? Have you developed strategies or techniques to enhance your focus in pursuit of your creative goals?*

7. *What lessons have you learned from your own experiences with focus and discipline that you believe can be applied to your creative endeavors today?*

8. *Think about the role of focus in the lives of other creative individuals, whether historical figures or contemporary artists. Are there examples that inspire you to further harness the power of focus?*

9. *Based on your reflections, what advice or insights would you offer to others who are striving to maintain focus amidst life's distractions?*

10. *Finally, consider how you can apply the lessons of focus to your current creative projects. What steps can you take to enhance your ability to stay focused on your creative goals?*

Admiral William H. McRaven

Admiral William H. McRaven, a retired US Navy SEAL, is a distinguished military leader renowned for his unwavering focus and remarkable contributions to US Special Operations. Born in Pinehurst, North Carolina, on November 6,1955, McRaven's journey to becoming a decorated admiral and national hero began with his early fascination with adventure and service. After graduating from the University of Texas at Austin with a degree in journalism, McRaven was commissioned as a US Navy SEAL officer in 1977. Throughout his military career, he consistently demonstrated an exceptional ability to concentrate on missions, even when faced with the most challenging and perilous circumstances.

One of McRaven's most iconic moments occurred during his tenure as the commander of US Special Operations Command (USSOCOM). He led Operation Neptune Spear, the daring mission that resulted in the capture of Osama bin Laden in 2011. This operation required meticulous planning, unparalleled precision, and extraordinary focus as the world watched with bated breath. Admiral McRaven's leadership philosophy centers on the concept of "Make Your Bed," which emphasizes the importance of accomplishing small tasks with precision and attention to detail. He authored a best-selling book, *Make Your Bed: Little Things That Can Change Your Life... And Maybe the World*, where he expands on this philosophy, showcasing how small acts of discipline and focus can lead to monumental achievements.

Beyond his military career, McRaven serves as a beacon of inspiration for leaders in all fields. His commitment to focus, discipline, and unwavering dedication to his missions have left an indelible mark on the world, demonstrating that extraordinary accomplishments are attainable through the power of unwavering focus. Admiral McRaven's life and career exemplify how focus, discipline, and dedication can enable individuals to conquer the most formidable challenges and serve as an enduring source of inspiration for those striving to achieve their own goals.

Marie Curie

Marie Curie—born Maria Sklodowska in Warsaw, Poland, on November 7, 1867—is a pioneering physicist and chemist celebrated for her groundbreaking work in the field of radioactivity. Her life story is a testament to the power of relentless focus and unwavering determination in the pursuit of scientific discovery. Despite facing significant barriers as a woman in the male-dominated scientific community of the late-nineteenth and early twentieth centuries, Curie's unyielding commitment to her work led to numerous breakthroughs.

She became the first woman to win a Nobel Prize and remains the only individual to have received Nobel Prizes in two different scientific fields. Curie's scientific journey began in Paris, where she studied physics and mathematics at the University of Paris (Sorbonne). It was there that she met Pierre Curie, a fellow scientist who would later become her husband and collaborator. Together, they embarked on pioneering research into radioactivity, discovering the elements polonium and radium. This work earned her the Nobel Prize in Physics in 1903, making her the first woman to receive this honor.

Marie Curie's relentless focus on her research extended beyond her scientific discoveries. During World War I, she established mobile radiography units, or "Petites Curies," to provide x-ray services to field hospitals, thereby revolutionizing medical diagnosis and treatment for wounded soldiers. Despite the physical toll of her research, which ultimately contributed to her premature death from radiation-related illnesses in 1934, Curie's legacy endures as an embodiment of dedication and unwavering focus in the face of adversity. Her pioneering work in radioactivity laid the foundation for countless scientific advancements, including the development of modern cancer treatments.

Marie Curie's story serves as an inspiration to all who seek to achieve greatness through their unwavering focus and dedication to their chosen path. Her remarkable life and groundbreaking scientific contributions continue to remind us of the boundless potential that can be unlocked when one remains committed to their passion and vision.

Michael Phelps

Michael Phelps—born on June 30, 1985, in Baltimore, Maryland—is a legendary swimmer and the most decorated Olympian of all time. His exceptional journey in the world of competitive swimming serves as a testament to the transformative power of focus and dedication. From a young age, Phelps displayed an affinity for the water. His early experiences in swimming competitions provided a glimpse of his extraordinary talent. Yet it was his unwavering commitment to the sport and unparalleled focus that set him on a path to greatness.

Phelps' rise to Olympic stardom culminated in the 2004 Athens Olympics when he won six gold and two bronze medals. This remarkable feat marked the beginning of a career that would redefine the possibilities of swimming. His ability to maintain a laser-like focus on his training, technique, and goals allowed him to set and break numerous world records.

The pinnacle of Phelps' career came at the 2008 Beijing Olympics, where he secured unprecedented eight gold medals in single games. This extraordinary achievement showcased his unmatched ability to stay composed under immense pressure and perform at the highest level when it mattered most. Phelps' journey was not without its challenges. He faced personal struggles and setbacks but always managed to regain his focus and determination.

His story is a testament to the power of resilience, perseverance, and unwavering concentration in the face of adversity. Beyond the pool, Phelps has become an advocate for mental health awareness, sharing his own experiences with depression and the importance of seeking help. His commitment to destigmatizing mental health issues highlights the significance of maintaining focus on well-being and personal growth.

Michael Phelps' life and athletic achievements exemplify how unwavering focus and dedication can lead to unparalleled success. His story inspires individuals from all walks of life to pursue their passions with relentless determination, showing that greatness is attainable through the power of unwavering concentration.

Malala Yousafzai

Malala Yousafzai—born on July 12, 1997, in Mingora, Pakistan—is a globally recognized education activist and the youngest-ever Nobel Prize laureate. Her remarkable journey is a testament to the indomitable power of focus and resilience in the pursuit of justice and education.

Malala's early life in Pakistan's Swat Valley was marked by her unwavering commitment to education in the face of growing adversity. As the Taliban's influence spread in the region, they sought to ban girls from attending school. Undeterred, Malala continued her education and became a vocal advocate for girls' right to learn. Her relentless focus on education and gender equality led her to speak out against the Taliban's oppressive regime, even at a young age.

In 2012, tragedy struck when Malala was targeted in an assassination attempt. She survived the attack, and her story captured the world's attention. Malala's unwavering determination to champion girls' education remained undiminished. She coauthored the memoir *I Am Malala*, which further amplified her message. In 2014, at the age of seventeen, she became the youngest recipient of the Nobel Peace Prize for her courageous advocacy.

Today, Malala is the cofounder of the Malala Fund, an organization dedicated to ensuring twelve years of free, safe, and quality education for girls around the world. Her relentless focus on this mission has led to tangible changes in educational access and opportunities for countless girls in impoverished and marginalized communities.

Malala's story serves as an inspiration to all who aspire to make a difference through unwavering focus and a commitment to justice. Her dedication to girls' education, even in the face of grave danger, demonstrates the extraordinary impact that can be achieved when one remains resolute in their pursuit of a better world. Malala Yousafzai's life and advocacy remind us that even the most daunting challenges can be overcome through unwavering focus and a steadfast commitment to a noble cause. Her story continues to inspire individuals worldwide to work tirelessly for positive change in their communities and the world at large.

Elon Musk

Elon Musk—born on June 28, 1971, in Pretoria, South Africa—is a visionary entrepreneur and innovator known for his transformative impact on multiple industries, including space exploration, electric vehicles, and renewable energy. His extraordinary journey exemplifies the power of unwavering focus and audacious goals in achieving groundbreaking advancements. From a young age, Musk displayed an insatiable curiosity and an unrelenting desire to make a difference in the world. He cofounded Zip2, an online business directory, which he sold for $307 million in 1999.

However, it was with the creation of companies like SpaceX, Tesla, and SolarCity that Musk truly demonstrated the potential of focus and determination. At SpaceX, Musk set out to reduce the cost of space travel and make it possible for humans to become a multi-planetary species. His commitment to this vision led to the development of reusable rockets and the successful launch of numerous missions, including those to the International Space Station. In the electric vehicle sector, Musk's relentless focus on sustainability and innovation catapulted Tesla into a global leader. Under his leadership, Tesla introduced electric cars that redefined the automotive industry and accelerated the transition to clean energy. Musk's work also extends to renewable energy solutions. Through SolarCity and the development of the Tesla Powerwall, he aimed to revolutionize how the world generates and consumes energy, reducing dependence on fossil fuels.

While Musk's endeavors have faced numerous challenges and skeptics, his unwavering focus on audacious goals and his ability to persevere in the face of adversity have been key to his success. His commitment to pushing the boundaries of technology and his determination to address pressing global issues, such as climate change, continue to inspire innovators and entrepreneurs worldwide. Elon Musk's life and achievements underscore the incredible potential of focus, ambition, and relentless determination in driving transformative change. His story serves as a beacon of inspiration for those who dare to dream big and remain steadfast in their pursuit of revolutionary ideas and solutions.

Simone Biles

Simone Biles—born on March 14, 1997, in Columbus, Ohio—is a world-renowned gymnast and Olympic gold medalist. Her extraordinary journey in the realm of gymnastics serves as a testament to the power of relentless focus, unwavering dedication, and unyielding determination.

From a young age, Biles exhibited exceptional talent and a natural affinity for gymnastics. Her early experiences in the sport foreshadowed a remarkable career marked by unprecedented success. Yet it was her unwavering commitment to mastering her craft that set her apart. Biles' rise to international prominence came at the 2016 Rio Olympics, where she secured four gold medals and one bronze. Her flawless routines and gravity-defying gymnastics routines left spectators and judges in awe. Her ability to maintain pinpoint focus during high-pressure situations is a hallmark of her career. What makes Biles' journey even more remarkable is her capacity to overcome adversity. She faced personal challenges, including the revelation of sexual abuse within the sport. Despite these difficulties, Biles remained steadfast in her commitment to gymnastics and her dedication to becoming the best in the world. Her pursuit of perfection in gymnastics has made her an icon in the sport and an inspiration to aspiring athletes worldwide.

Beyond her accomplishments, Simone Biles serves as a vocal advocate for mental health awareness. Her openness about her struggles and her focus on self-care emphasize the importance of maintaining focus not only on athletic excellence but also on well-being. Simone Biles' life story showcases how unwavering focus, boundless dedication, and the pursuit of excellence can lead to unparalleled success. Her remarkable journey continues to inspire athletes, artists, and individuals in all walks of life to pursue their passions and dreams with unwavering determination and concentration.

Exercise: The Focus Meditation: Incorporate meditation into your daily routine to enhance your focus. Follow these steps to practice The Focus Meditation:

1. ***Find a quiet space:*** Choose a serene and quiet place where you won't be disturbed. Sit comfortably in a chair or on a cushion with your back straight.

2. ***Set a timer:*** Use a timer to ensure you dedicate a specific amount of time to this practice. Start with a manageable duration, like ten minutes, and gradually extend it as you become more comfortable.

3. ***Close your eyes:*** Gently close your eyes to eliminate external distractions. Take a few deep breaths to relax your body and clear your mind.

4. ***Focus on your breath:*** Direct your attention to your breath. Notice the sensation of the air entering and leaving

your nostrils or the rise and fall of your chest and abdomen as you breathe.

5. **Count your breaths:** As you continue to breathe, count each breath from one to ten. When you reach ten, start again from one. If your mind wanders or you lose count, gently bring your focus back to the breath and start over.

6. **Mindfulness of thoughts:** As thoughts, distractions, or sensations arise, acknowledge them without judgment, and then gently return your focus to your breath and counting.

7. **Deepen your focus:** As you practice regularly, you'll find it easier to maintain your concentration. Gradually increase the count to twenty or thirty, challenging your ability to sustain focus.

Tying the spiritual with the physical

Incorporating focus-enhancing practices, like meditation into your daily routine, can bridge the gap between the spiritual and the physical aspects of creativity.
Here's how:

1. **Mind-body connection:** Meditation fosters a deep connection between your mind and body. As you focus on your breath and count, you become aware of the physical sensations associated with your thoughts and emotions. This heightened awareness can translate into a greater understanding of the physical and emotional aspects of your creative process.

2. **Clarity of purpose:** Through regular meditation, you can gain clarity about your creative goals and the deeper spiritual purpose behind your artistic endeavors. As you elim-

inate distractions and cultivate inner stillness, you may uncover profound insights that guide your creative journey.

3. *Enhanced concentration:* The practice of meditation strengthens your ability to concentrate, not only during your sessions but also in your creative work. Whether you're writing, painting, or composing, the improved focus gained from meditation allows you to immerse yourself more deeply in your art.

4. *Emotional resilience:* Meditation equips you with emotional resilience, enabling you to navigate creative challenges and setbacks with greater composure. This spiritual and emotional grounding can help you stay committed to your artistic vision, even in the face of adversity.

By incorporating meditation into your life, you'll discover how it can harmonize the spiritual and physical dimensions of your creative journey. It provides a valuable tool for enhancing focus, deepening self-awareness, and connecting with the inner wellspring of inspiration that fuels your artistic endeavors.

Closing message

As we conclude this chapter on "The Power of Focus," we are reminded of the profound impact that unwavering concentration can have on our lives. The stories of Admiral William H. McRaven, Marie Curie, Michael Phelps, Malala Yousafzai, Elon Musk, and Simone Biles serve as beacons of inspiration, illuminating the path to greatness through relentless dedication. Through their journeys, we've witnessed how focus can turn audacious dreams into reality, transform adversity into opportunity, and elevate one's pursuit of excellence. These remarkable individuals have shown us that focus is not just a tool; it is a superpower that can shape destinies, change the world, and leave an indelible mark on humanity. In our fast-paced world, where distractions abound, the ability to harness this super-power is more crucial than ever. By practicing the art of concentration through meditation and nurturing our mind-body connection, we unlock the door to a deeper understanding of our creative selves. Let us carry forward the wisdom of these extraordinary individuals as a guiding light in our own pursuits. Let us cultivate unwavering focus, embrace audacious goals, and face challenges with resilience. In doing so, we tap into our own reservoirs of potential and discover that, like them, we too possess the power to achieve greatness.

Now as we turn the page to explore "The Fire of Passion" in Chapter 8, remember this: Your journey is a canvas, and your focus is the brush that paints your masterpiece. With each stroke of concentration, you bring your vision to life. Embrace this superpower, for it is your key to unlocking the infinite potential within.

Closing quotes

> *The successful warrior is the average man, with laser-like focus. (Bruce Lee)*

> *The future depends on what you do today. (Mahatma Gandhi)*

> *Your ability to focus will determine your ability to succeed in life. (Anonymous)*

> *The secret of change is to focus all your energy not on fighting the old, but on building the new. (Socrates)*

> *The power of concentration is the only key to the treasure house of knowledge. (Swami Vivekananda)*

With focus as your ally, you hold the key to unlocking your creative genius and shaping your destiny. Onward to the fire of passion in Chapter 8, where we explore how deep-seated love for your craft can ignite extraordinary creativity.

8

The Fire of Passion

In the depths of one's soul lies a wellspring of passion, an unquenchable fire that can ignite the extraordinary. In this chapter, we embark on a journey through the flames of creativity, exploring the power of passion as a God-given superpower.

In the heart of every child, there exists a burning passion, a fire that can illuminate the darkest of paths and fuel the most audacious dreams. As a young boy, I felt that fire, a fervent desire to step into the ring, to become a wrestler, and to follow in the footsteps of my heroes—Hulk Hogan, Bret Hart, Shawn Michaels. Their charisma, their larger-than-life presence, ignited my passion, and the excitement of the squared circle pulsed through my veins. But as life unfolded and I journeyed into adulthood, my passions shifted, and the ring gave way to a different kind of stage—one adorned with the spotlight of the arts. It was a choice that demanded unwavering resolve, a decision to pursue a path less traveled. Yet in that transition, I discovered the enduring power of passion and its ability to reshape destinies. Throughout history, there have been those whose flames of passion blazed so brightly that they altered the course of nations and inspired generations.

One such figure, a beacon of unwavering zeal, was Joan of Arc. Her story, like mine and countless others, bears witness to the transformative potential of unbridled passion. Join me as we delve into the heart of "The Fire of Passion" in this chapter. Together, we will explore the fervor that fueled the likes of Joan of Arc and discover how our own passions, though they may evolve, remain a powerful force in our creative journeys. Let us be inspired by history's most passionate souls as we rekindle our own flames and let them illuminate the path to boundless creativity.

Joan of Arc: The divine flame

In the fifteenth century, amidst the turmoil of the Hundred Years' War, a young peasant girl from Domrémy, France, emerged as a living embodiment of passion's might. Joan of Arc, driven by an unwavering conviction and fervent belief, heard the divine call to liberate her homeland from English occupation. Her fervor was a beacon that illuminated the darkest of times. Joan's passion was unlike any other as she rallied armies, inspired a nation, and defied the conventions of her time. Driven by a divine purpose, she donned armor and led troops into battle, despite being just a teenager. Her passion was her compass, guiding her through the chaos of war and the skepticism of her peers. In the face of adversity, Joan's unyielding flame burned brighter, transcending mortal limitations.

Passion's role in my creative odyssey

As my own life's path veered from the wrestling ring to the stage and screen, the essence of passion remained a constant companion. The passion that once fueled my dreams of becoming a wrestler seamlessly transitioned into my pursuits in the arts. I discovered that passion was not confined to a singular endeavor but could transform, expand, and enrich our creative journey.

Acting, comedy, writing—each step in my artistic odyssey was illuminated by the fiery beacon of passion. It was the force that propelled me forward, even in the face of challenges. Through the ups and downs of the entertainment industry, my passion remained unwavering, a guiding star in the constellation of creativity.

The creative alchemy of passion

Passion has the remarkable power to transmute ordinary actions into extraordinary expressions. It infuses every brushstroke of an artist's masterpiece, every note of a composer's symphony, and every word of a writer's tale with an otherworldly vitality. The essence of passion transforms mere mortals into conduits of the divine, allowing them to channel inspiration and spark revolutions of the heart and mind. In this chapter, we will delve deep into the cauldron of creativity, exploring how passion can transform the ordinary into the extraordinary. We will unveil the alchemy of passion that turns leaden moments into golden memories and how it guides us toward our true purpose.

Passion and self-discovery

Passion is not solely an external force; it is a journey of self-discovery. It invites us to explore the innermost chambers of our hearts and minds, to uncover our true callings, and to align our creative work with our deepest desires. Just as Joan of Arc discovered her divine mission, we too can find purpose and meaning through the flames of our passions. Throughout this chapter, we will share personal anecdotes, revealing how passion has been the driving force behind our creative pursuits. We will discuss practical ways to reconnect with your own passions and infuse them into your creative endeavors. Together, we will unlock the transformative potential of unwavering dedication to what sets your soul ablaze.

Lesser-known torchbearers of passion

As we explore the theme of passion, we will introduce you to lesser-known artists whose fervor ignited unique and groundbreaking contributions to the arts. Their stories serve as a reminder that passion, regardless of recognition or fame, can lead to extraordinary creativity and leave an indelible mark on the world.

Exercise: Igniting Your Creative Passion: Embarking on a journey to reignite your creative passion can be a transformative experience. Try this exercise to reconnect with your deepest passions:

1. *Reflect on your childhood:* Recall the activities or interests that brought you immense joy during your childhood. Whether it was painting, writing stories, playing an instrument, or simply daydreaming, these childhood passions often provide clues to your true creative inclinations.

2. *Create a passion collage:* Collect magazines, images, or words that resonate with you and your creative aspirations. Assemble them into a collage that visually represents your passions and artistic desires. This tactile exercise can help you tap into your subconscious desires.

3. *Rediscover old interests:* Revisit hobbies or interests you once loved but may have set aside. Whether it's playing a musical instrument, dancing, cooking, or gardening, reengaging with these activities can reignite the spark of passion.

4. *Engage with art:* Attend art exhibitions, concerts, or performances that align with your interests. Immerse yourself in the creativity of others to reignite your own artistic enthusiasm.

5. *Daily creative ritual:* Dedicate a specific time each day, even if it's just fifteen minutes, to engage in a creative pursuit. Whether you write in a journal, sketch, or practice a musical instrument, consistent action can reignite your creative flame.

6. ***Seek inspiration:*** Read biographies or autobiographies of passionate individuals who have made a mark in your field of interest. Discover the challenges they faced and how their unwavering commitment to their craft fueled their success.

7. ***Share your passion:*** Collaborate with others who share your interests or take a class related to your passion. Sharing experiences and ideas can be a powerful catalyst for creativity.

Now let's delve into the lives of passionate individuals who blazed trails with their unwavering commitment to their callings.

Ella Fitzgerald: The Queen of Jazz

Ella Fitzgerald, born in 1917, was a jazz icon whose passion for music transcended generations. Her mesmerizing voice and remarkable improvisational skills made her one of the most influential jazz vocalists of all time. Ella's passion for music began as a young girl, and she honed her craft in the midst of adversity. Despite facing racial discrimination and personal challenges, Ella's unwavering commitment to her art led to groundbreaking performances at prestigious venues and collaborations with jazz legends like Duke Ellington and Louis Armstrong. Her passion for music not only defined her career but also left an indelible mark on the world of jazz.

Vincent van Gogh: The Starry Night's *creator*

Vincent van Gogh's passionate pursuit of art is a testament to the transformative power of creative fervor. Born in 1853, this Dutch Postimpressionist painter created some of the most celebrated and emotionally charged artworks in history. Vincent's passion for painting ignited during his late twenties, and he produced over two thousand works of art in just a decade. Driven by an insatiable desire to capture the essence of life and emotions through his paintings, Vincent's bold use of color and expressive brushwork continue to captivate art enthusiasts worldwide. His passion for art was so intense that he once said, "I would rather die of passion than of boredom." Vincent's legacy reminds us that embracing our passions can lead to artistic brilliance and profound self-discovery.

Amelia Earhart: Soaring into the skies

Amelia Earhart, a pioneer of aviation born in 1897, was a trailblazer whose passion for flying reached unprecedented heights. From the moment she first took to the skies, Earhart's heart was forever captured by the freedom and exhilaration of flight. Her relentless determination to break gender barriers in aviation knew no bounds. Despite the prevailing gender biases of her era, Amelia soared above adversity. Her passion for aviation led her to become the first woman to fly solo across the Atlantic Ocean. Her courage and unwavering commitment to her craft made her an inspiration to aspiring aviators, and her legacy continues to empower women in aviation today.

Ludwig van Beethoven: The music of the soul

Ludwig van Beethoven, born in 1770, was a composer whose passionate compositions transcended mere notes and became an expression of the human soul. His journey into the world of music began at a young age, and his passion for composing was evident even in the face of personal hardship. Beethoven's dedication to his craft was unwavering, even as he battled deafness. His passion for music fueled the creation of some of the most celebrated symphonies and sonatas in history, including the iconic "Ninth Symphony." Beethoven's story reminds us that true passion can overcome adversity and allow us to create beauty even in the face of challenges.

Exercise: The Passion Playlist: Create a playlist of songs that resonate with your passions. Whether it's the lyrics, melodies, or rhythms, these songs should evoke the emotions and desires associated with what you're most passionate about. Whenever you need a boost of inspiration, listen to your Passion Playlist to reignite your creative fervor.

1. *What songs instantly lift your spirits and make you feel energized?*

2. *Are there specific lyrics that resonate deeply with your passions or creative aspirations?*

3. *Do you associate certain melodies or rhythms with your creative work or hobbies?*

4. *Have you ever had a song that inspired a moment of clarity or a breakthrough in your creative process?*

5. *Are there artists or bands whose music aligns closely with your passions or the themes of your creative work?*

6. *Do you have a favorite song that motivates you to overcome challenges and keep pursuing your creative goals?*

7. *Are there songs that you find particularly soothing or calming, which help you focus during creative sessions?*

8. *Have you ever used music as a source of inspiration when brainstorming ideas or working on creative projects?*

9. *Are there songs that transport you to a specific time or place associated with your passions?*

10. *What emotions do you feel when you listen to your chosen songs, and how do these emotions relate to your creative journey?*

Remember, your "Passion Playlist" should be a reflection of your innermost passions and creative desires. Use these questions to guide your song selection and create a playlist that ignites your creative flame whenever you listen to it. As you engage in the "Passion Portrait" exercise and curate your Passion Playlist, let these stories serve as a reminder that your passions are not mere whims; they are the keys to unlocking your boundless creativity. In the next section, we will explore the connection between patience and the creative process, delving into "The Wisdom of Patience." This chapter will reveal how patience can be a superpower in nurturing and refining your artistic endeavors.

Exercise: The Passion Portrait: Create a visual representation of your own passions through art. Use any medium you prefer—paint, sketch, collage, or digital tools. Let your imagination run wild as you depict your passions and desires. This exercise is not about perfection but about capturing the essence of what truly inspires you. Display your Passion Portrait as a reminder of your creative journey's renewed spark. Creating a Passion Portrait is a deeply personal and visual exercise that allows you to represent your passions and creative desires. Here are some questions to help you get started on your Passion Portrait:

1. *What are the core passions and creative pursuits that drive you in life?*

2. *Can you recall specific moments or memories associated with these passions that stand out in your mind?*

3. *Are there symbols or visual elements that represent your passions, such as musical notes, art supplies, or nature imagery?*

4. *What colors evoke the emotions and energy of your passions? Are there specific colors that come to mind when you think about your creative work?*

5. *Are there words, phrases, or quotes that resonate with your passions and can be incorporated into your Passion Portrait?*

6. *Do you have any personal mantras or affirmations related to your creative journey that you'd like to include?*

7. *Are there images or photos that hold significance for you in connection with your passions and creative endeavors?*

8. *How would you describe the overall mood or atmosphere you want your Passion Portrait to convey?*

9. *What materials or artistic mediums do you feel most drawn to for creating your visual representation of passion?*

10. *How do you envision your Passion Portrait serving as a source of inspiration and motivation in your creative space?*

These questions can guide your creative process as you assemble your Passion Portrait. Remember that there are no right or wrong answers in this exercise—it's all about expressing your unique passions and creative aspirations through visual art.

1. *Passion Journaling*

What is it? Passion journaling is a structured practice of recording your thoughts, ideas, and experiences related to your creative passions in a dedicated journal or digital document. It serves as a dynamic space for self-discovery, goal setting, and creative exploration.
How to do it:

1.   Select a journal that resonates with you, whether it's a physical notebook, a digital journaling app, or a dedicated section in your existing journal.
2.   **Set a routine:** Establish a consistent journaling routine. Dedicate a specific time each day or week to reflect on your creative passions. This regular practice will help you stay connected to your aspirations.
3.   **Write freely:** Approach journaling as a judgment-free zone. Write whatever comes to mind, whether it's ideas for a project, reflections on your progress, or the emotions and challenges you face in pursuing your passions.
4.   **Goal setting:** Use your passion journal to set clear, actionable goals related to your creative endeavors. Break larger goals into smaller, achievable steps, and track your progress over time.
5.   **Creative brainstorming:** When inspiration strikes, capture it in your journal. Jot down new project ideas, concepts, or even doodles that spring to mind. Your journal can become a repository of creative sparks waiting to be ignited.
6.   **Reflect and evaluate:** Regularly review your journal entries to reflect on your creative journey. Consider what's working well, what challenges you're encountering, and how your passions are evolving.
7.   **Express gratitude:** Use your passion journal to express gratitude for the opportunities, experiences, and insights your

creative pursuits have brought into your life. Gratitude can fuel your passion.

Why it matters:

- **Clarity and Focus:** Passion journaling helps clarify your creative goals and aspirations, allowing you to focus your energy on what truly matters to you.
- **Accountability:** By documenting your progress and setting goals, you hold yourself accountable for your creative endeavors. By documenting your progress and setting goals, you hold yourself accountable for your creative endeavors.
- **Creative growth:** As you reflect on your journey, you gain insights into your creative process, allowing you to adapt, refine, and grow as an artist or creator.
- **Inspiration repository:** Your journal becomes a treasure trove of ideas and inspirations, providing a wellspring of creativity when you need it most.
- **Self-discovery:** Journaling enables you to explore your passions on a deeper level, uncovering new facets of yourself and your creative potential.

Remember, there's no right or wrong way to journal about your passions. It's a personal practice that evolves with you. Over time, your passion journal can become a valuable companion on your creative journey, offering guidance, motivation, and a space for your creative spirit to flourish. These passionate individuals, from Ella Fitzgerald's enchanting melodies to Vincent van Gogh's vibrant canvases, serve as beacons of inspiration. Their unwavering commitment to their callings illustrates that passion is the driving force behind enduring creativity. As we proceed on our journey, let their stories remind us that our own passions, once reignited, can lead to remarkable artistic endeavors and profound self-discovery.

2. *Passion mind mapping*

What is it? Passion mind mapping is a visual technique that helps you explore, organize, and expand upon your creative passions. It's a dynamic way to connect ideas and delve into the intricacies of your interests.

How to do it:

1. ***Start with a central passion:*** In the center of a blank page or digital canvas, write or draw your central passion. This could be a broad category like "writing," "music," or "visual art."
2. ***Branch out:*** Create branches radiating from the central passion. Each branch represents a subcategory, project, or aspect of your central passion. For example, if your central passion is "writing," branches might include "poetry," "fiction," "journalism," and so on.
3. ***Detail subcategories:*** Expand on each subcategory by adding more branches or nodes. For instance, under "fiction writing," you might have branches for "historical fiction," "fantasy," and "science fiction."
4. ***Explore connections:*** As you expand your mind map, look for connections and intersections between different subcategories. These connections can lead to new ideas and creative projects.
5. ***Add keywords and concepts:*** Along each branch, include keywords, concepts, or short descriptions that capture what each subcategory or project entails. These serve as prompts for further exploration.
6. ***Visual elements:*** Incorporate visuals like sketches, symbols, or images that represent each subcategory or project. Visual elements can make your mind map more engaging and memorable.
7. ***Color coding:*** Consider using colors to differentiate between branches or to highlight areas of particular interest or priority.

8. ***Regular updates:*** Your passion mind map is a dynamic tool. Update it as your passions evolve, new interests emerge, or as you make progress on creative projects.

Why it matters:

- ***Visualization:*** Mind mapping provides a clear and visual representation of your creative passions, making it easier to see the big picture.
- ***Organization:*** It helps you organize your thoughts, projects, and interests in a structured way.
- ***Creative exploration:*** Mind mapping encourages you to explore related and interconnected areas of interest that you might not have considered otherwise.
- ***Inspiration generation:*** By visually connecting different elements, you can generate new ideas and creative projects.
- ***Focus:*** Mind maps can help you prioritize and focus your creative efforts on the areas that resonate most with you. Passion mind mapping is a creative exercise that not only helps you understand your passions but also enables you to see how they interconnect and evolve. It's a tool for creative exploration and strategy that can guide you on your artistic journey.

3. *Passion collage*

What is it? A passion collage is a visual representation of your creative passions and aspirations created by compiling images, words, symbols, and artistic elements that resonate with your interests.
How to do it:

1. ***Gather materials:*** Collect magazines, newspapers, printouts, photographs, drawings, or any visual materials that you feel represent your passions or inspire your creative pursuits.

2. ***Create a mood board:*** Use a large sheet of paper, poster board, canvas, or even a digital platform to create your passion collage.

3. ***Select key themes:*** Identify the key themes or areas of passion you want to focus on within your collage. These could be broad categories like "writing," "music," "travel," or specific projects or goals.

4. ***Begin assembling:*** Cut out images, words, and symbols from your collected materials that align with your chosen themes. Arrange them on your canvas in a visually appealing and meaningful way.

5. ***Add personal touch:*** Consider adding personal elements, such as your own drawings, photographs, or handwritten notes that convey your unique connection to your passions.

6. ***Layer and overlap:*** Experiment with layering and overlapping elements to create depth and complexity in your collage. This can represent the multifaceted nature of your passions.

7. ***Use colors:*** Utilize colors that evoke the emotions and energy associated with your creative pursuits. Color choices can influence the overall mood of your collage.

8. ***Reflect and adjust:*** Take breaks to step back and reflect on your collage's progress. Make adjustments as needed to ensure it resonates with your artistic vision.

9. ***Seal and display:*** Once your passion collage is complete, consider sealing it with a clear adhesive or laminating it to preserve your work. Display it prominently in your creative space for daily inspiration.

Why it matters:

- ***Visual inspiration:*** A passion collage serves as a constant source of visual inspiration, reminding you of your creative passions and goals.

- *Clarity:* Creating a collage can help clarify and refine your creative aspirations by distilling them into tangible images and words.
- *Visualization:* It provides a visual representation of your creative vision, making it easier to connect with and manifest your desires.
- *Motivation:* Viewing your passion collage regularly can motivate you to take action and pursue your creative endeavors with renewed enthusiasm.
- *Personal connection:* A passion collage is deeply personal, reflecting your unique interests, dreams, and desires. A passion collage is a tactile and artistic way to connect with your creative passions on a visceral level. It serves as a powerful reminder of your artistic goals and can infuse your creative space with a sense of purpose and inspiration.

4. *Passion vision board*

What is it? A passion vision board is a visual representation of your creative passions, goals, and aspirations. Unlike a traditional collage, a vision board is typically more goal-oriented, focusing on what you want to achieve in your creative journey.
How to do it:

1. *Gather supplies:* Collect magazines, newspapers, print-outs, photographs, art supplies, scissors, glue, a corkboard, poster board, or a digital platform if creating a virtual vision board.
2. *Define your goals:* Clearly define your creative goals and aspirations. What do you want to achieve in your artistic journey? Be specific about projects, milestones, or skills you want to acquire.
3. *Gather visuals:* Look for images, words, and symbols that align with your creative goals. These visuals should represent what you want to manifest in your artistic life.

4. *Organize by categories:* Divide your vision board into categories that reflect different aspects of your creative journey. For example, you could have sections for "writing goals," "artistic skills," or "career achievements."

5. *Arrange your vision:* Begin arranging the visuals on your vision board. Place them strategically within each category, focusing on what matters most to you. Consider the layout and flow of your board.

6. *Add personal touch:* Include personal elements like photographs of your own artwork, handwritten notes outlining your goals, or drawings that represent your unique creative style.

7. *Visualize success:* As you place visuals on your vision board, imagine yourself achieving these goals. Feel the emotions and excitement associated with your creative accomplishments.

8. *Affirmations:* Incorporate positive affirmations or motivational quotes that resonate with your artistic journey. These can reinforce your belief in your creative abilities.

9. *Reflect and update:* Regularly reflect on your vision board to stay focused on your creative aspirations. Update it as you achieve goals or as your artistic path evolves.

10. *Display your vision:* Place your vision board where you can see it daily, whether it's in your workspace, bedroom, or a digital background. Regularly connecting with your vision reinforces your commitment.

Why it matters:

- *Goal alignment:* A vision board helps align your creative goals with your visual aspirations, making them more tangible and achievable.
- *Visualization:* Regularly viewing your vision board allows you to vividly visualize your creative success, which can boost motivation and confidence.

- *Focus and clarity:* It provides clarity on your artistic direction and serves as a reminder of your purpose and passions.
- *Manifestation:* Many believe that the act of visualizing your goals through a vision board can help manifest them into reality.
- *Tracking progress:* As you achieve goals, your vision board serves as a record of your creative journey and a source of pride and inspiration. Creating a passion vision board is a proactive way to turn your creative dreams into actionable goals. It not only keeps your artistic aspirations at the forefront of your mind but also empowers you to take deliberate steps toward achieving them.

5. *Passion meditation*

What is it? Passion meditation is a mindfulness practice that focuses on your creative passions and aspirations. It involves harnessing the power of your mind to visualize, connect with, and energize your creative desires.
How to do it:

1. *Find a quiet space:* Choose a quiet and comfortable space where you won't be disturbed during your meditation.
2. *Relax your body:* Sit or lie down in a relaxed posture. Close your eyes and take a few deep breaths to calm your body and mind.
3. *Focus on your breath:* Pay attention to your breath as it enters and leaves your body. Let go of any tension with each exhale.
4. *Set your intention:* State your intention for the meditation, which is to connect with your creative passions and aspirations.
5. *Visualize your creative desires:* In your mind's eye, start to visualize your creative passions. Imagine yourself fully engaged in your creative pursuits, whether it's writing, painting, music, or any other form of art.

6. **Feel the emotions:** As you visualize your passions, allow yourself to feel the emotions associated with them. Feel the joy, excitement, and fulfillment that your creative endeavors bring.

7. **Connect with your goals:** Mentally connect with your creative goals and aspirations. Visualize achieving these goals and savor the sense of accomplishment.

8. **Positive affirmations:** Repeat positive affirmations related to your passions. For example, "I am a creative force," or "I am capable of bringing my artistic visions to life."

9. **Deepen the visualization:** Go deeper into your creative visualization. Imagine the details, colors, sounds, and sensations associated with your creative process.

10. **Express gratitude:** Take a moment to express gratitude for your creative talents, opportunities, and the experiences that have shaped your artistic journey.

11. **Transition back:** Slowly transition back to the present moment. Wiggle your fingers and toes, and when you're ready, open your eyes.

12. **Reflect:** After your meditation, spend a few moments reflecting on the emotions and insights that arose during the practice. Consider any new ideas or inspirations.

Why it matters:

- **Emotional alignment:** Passion meditation aligns your emotions with your creative aspirations, creating a positive and motivating mindset.

- **Visualization:** It helps you vividly visualize your creative success, making it more achievable.

- **Stress reduction:** Meditation is known for reducing stress and anxiety, allowing you to approach your creative pursuits with a calm and focused mind.

- **Connection to purpose:** By connecting with your passions through meditation, you strengthen your sense of purpose and dedication to your creative path.

- *Inspiration:* Passion meditation can spark new ideas and inspirations, enriching your creative process. Passion meditation is a powerful practice that connects you deeply with your creative desires and empowers you to move forward with purpose and enthusiasm. Regularly incorporating this practice into your routine can enhance your creative journey and foster a strong sense of alignment with your passions.

6. *Passion interviews*

What is it? Passion interviews involve engaging in conversations with fellow artists, creators, or individuals who share your creative passions. These interviews provide an opportunity to exchange ideas, gain insights, and find inspiration through collaborative discussions.
How to do it:

1. *Identify passionate peers:* Reach out to people in your creative network or online communities who share your creative interests. Look for individuals whose work or experiences inspire you.
2. *Schedule interviews:* Contact potential interviewees and propose the idea of a passion interview. Explain that you'd like to discuss their creative journey, insights, and experiences related to your shared passions.
3. *Prepare questions:* Prepare a list of open-ended questions that delve into their creative process, challenges, sources of inspiration, and personal insights. Tailor your questions to the specific passion or field of interest.
4. *Conduct the interview:* Schedule a time for the interview, whether it's in person, over the phone, via video call, or through written correspondence. Ensure a comfortable and respectful atmosphere.
5. *Listen actively:* During the interview, actively listen to the interviewee's responses. Encourage them to share their unique perspectives and stories.

6. *Engage in a dialogue:* Use the interview as an opportunity for a genuine exchange of ideas. Share your own experiences and insights when relevant, fostering a collaborative and supportive discussion.

7. *Take notes:* Record key takeaways, memorable quotes, and valuable advice from the interview. These notes can serve as a source of ongoing inspiration.

8. *Express gratitude:* After the interview, express your gratitude to the interviewee for their time and insights. Acknowledge the value they've added to your creative journey.

9. *Reflect:* Reflect on the interview and consider how the insights and experiences shared by your interviewee can inform and enrich your own creative pursuits.

10. *Share insights:* If appropriate and with permission, share the interview or highlights from it with your creative community. This can inspire others and foster a sense of connection.

Why it matters:

- *Diverse perspectives:* Passion interviews expose you to diverse perspectives, approaches, and ideas within your creative field.

- *Inspiration and motivation:* Hearing about the creative journeys and successes of others can serve as a powerful source of inspiration and motivation.

- *Community Building:* Engaging with fellow creatives fosters a sense of community and connection, reducing feelings of isolation on your artistic journey.

- *Shared learning:* Interviews provide an opportunity for shared learning, where both you and the interviewee can gain insights and knowledge from one another.

- *Collaboration:* Passion interviews can lead to potential collaborations, partnerships, or joint creative projects with like-minded individuals. By actively engaging in passion interviews, you not only gain valuable insights and inspiration but also contribute to building a supportive and interconnected creative community. These conversations can become a wellspring of creativity and shared enthusiasm for your artistic pursuits.

7. *Passion artistic challenge*

What is it? A passion artistic challenge is a creative exercise designed to push your boundaries, encourage experimentation, and reignite your artistic spark. It prompts you to explore new techniques, themes, or mediums related to your passions.
How to do it:

1. ***Select a challenge:*** Choose a specific challenge related to your creative passion. This could be a writing challenge, an art challenge, a musical challenge, or any other form of creative challenge.
2. ***Set clear parameters:*** Define the rules and parameters of the challenge. For example, if you're a writer, you might set a word count goal, a theme, or a time frame for completing a short story.
3. ***Choose a focus:*** Decide on the specific aspect of your passion you want to explore. If you're a visual artist, you might focus on a new painting technique or a different subject matter.
4. ***Plan and prepare:*** Gather the necessary materials or resources to undertake the challenge. This might involve acquiring new tools, research, or reference materials.
5. ***Get started:*** Begin the challenge with enthusiasm and an open mind. Allow yourself to embrace the process without excessive self-criticism.
6. ***Document your progress:*** Keep a journal or create a blog, vlog, or social media account to document your progress throughout the challenge. Share your journey with others if you feel comfortable.

7. **Embrace mistakes:** Don't be afraid to make mistakes or encounter difficulties. Challenges are meant to stretch your creative abilities and foster growth.
8. **Reflect and learn:** After completing the challenge, take time to reflect on what you've learned, the skills you've developed, and the insights you've gained.
9. **Apply what you've learned:** Incorporate the knowledge and skills acquired during the challenge into your ongoing creative pursuits. These experiences can enrich your work.
10. **Repeat or create new challenges:** Continue to challenge yourself regularly. You can either repeat the same challenge to deepen your expertise or create new challenges to explore different aspects of your passion.

Why it matters:

- **Growth and development:** Artistic challenges push you to grow and develop as a creative individual. They encourage you to step out of your comfort zone.
- **Inspiration:** Challenges can be a wellspring of inspiration, often leading to new ideas, projects, or directions in your creative journey.
- **Skill enhancement:** You have the opportunity to enhance your skills and explore new techniques or approaches related to your passion.
- **Self-expression:** Artistic challenges provide a platform for self-expression and experimentation, allowing you to express your creative voice more authentically.
- **Motivation:** Completing challenges can boost your motivation and sense of accomplishment, rekindling your passion for your chosen creative field.

8. *Passion reflection journal*

What is it? A passion reflection journal is a dedicated space where you can regularly reflect on your creative passions, experiences, challenges, and inspirations. It's a personal repository of insights and observations related to your artistic journey.

How to do it:

1. **Select a journal:** Choose a physical notebook, a digital journaling app, or any preferred medium for your reflection journal.
2. **Set a schedule:** Establish a regular schedule for journaling. This could be daily, weekly, or whenever you feel the need to reflect on your creative passions.
3. **Start with prompts:** Begin your journaling sessions with prompts or questions that encourage introspection. Some examples include: "What inspired me creatively today?" "What challenges did I encounter in my artistic pursuits?" "What progress have I made toward my creative goals?" "How can I overcome creative blocks or obstacles?" "What new ideas or projects am I excited about?"
4. **Write freely:** Allow your thoughts and feelings to flow freely onto the pages. Don't worry about grammar or structure; this is a space for raw, unfiltered expression.
5. **Explore emotions:** Pay attention to your emotions as you write. Explore why certain creative experiences or challenges evoke specific feelings.
6. **Document milestones:** Record significant milestones or achievements in your creative journey. Celebrate your successes, no matter how small.
7. **Express gratitude:** Take time to express gratitude for the opportunities, experiences, and individuals that have enriched your creative path.
8. **Set goals:** Outline your short-term and long-term creative goals. Define actionable steps to move closer to these goals.
9. **Reflect on growth:** Periodically review your journal entries to track your personal and creative growth. Identify patterns, recurring themes, and areas where you've evolved.

10. **Seek inspiration:** Use your reflection journal as a source of inspiration. Revisit past entries when you're in need of motivation or creative direction.

11. **Visual elements:** If you enjoy visual creativity, consider incorporating sketches, doodles, or collages into your journal to complement your written reflections.

Why it matters:

- **Self-awareness:** A passion reflection journal fosters self-awareness by helping you understand your creative motivations, challenges, and aspirations.

- **Progress tracking:** It serves as a tool for tracking your artistic progress, from the early stages of your journey to your ongoing growth and development.

- **Problem-solving:** Journaling can aid in problem-solving by allowing you to explore creative blocks or obstacles from different angles.

- **Emotional release:** Writing about your creative experiences can serve as a healthy emotional release, helping you process and cope with challenges.

- **Inspiration archive:** Over time, your journal becomes an archive of inspiration, offering a rich source of ideas and insights to draw from in your creative pursuits. A passion reflection journal is a personal sanctuary for your creative thoughts and feelings. Regularly engaging in reflective writing can deepen your connection to your artistic passions, enhance self-awareness, and provide a valuable resource for navigating your creative journey.

Participating in passion artistic challenges is an effective way to infuse excitement and growth into your creative journey. These challenges offer a structured and invigorating approach to exploring and evolving within your artistic pursuits.

9. Passion playlist creation

What is it? Creating a passion playlist is a musical journey that connects your creative passions with the power of music. It involves curating a collection of songs that inspire, energize, and evoke emotions related to your creative pursuits.

How to do it:

1. ***Choose a music platform:*** Select a music platform or app where you can create playlists. Popular choices include Spotify, Apple Music, YouTube, or even a dedicated playlist in your preferred music player.
2. ***Identify themes:*** Define the themes or emotions associated with your creative passions. For example, if you're a writer, your themes might include "imagination," "adventure," or "introspection."
3. ***Curate songs:*** Begin curating songs that align with your chosen themes. These songs can be from various genres and artists; focus on how they make you feel rather than their specific styles.
4. ***Build a narrative:*** Organize the songs to create a narrative or emotional journey within your playlist. Start with an opening track that sets the tone and gradually build to a climax.
5. ***Include personal favorites:*** Add songs that hold personal significance in your creative journey. These could be tracks that were playing during a pivotal moment or songs that resonate with your artistic identity.
6. ***Explore new music:*** Use this opportunity to discover new music that resonates with your passions. Seek out artists or songs that you haven't explored before but fit the themes you've chosen.
7. ***Name your playlist:*** Give your playlist a meaningful name that reflects its purpose, such as "Creative Flow," "Passion Unleashed," or "Artistic Inspiration."

8. *Listen mindfully:* When you listen to your passion play-list, do so mindfully. Pay attention to how the music makes you feel and how it enhances your creative mindset.

9. *Use it as a tool:* Incorporate your passion playlist into your creative routine. Listen to it while you work on your artistic projects, during brainstorming sessions, or when you need an extra dose of inspiration.

10. *Update and expand:* Periodically update and expand your passion playlist as you discover new songs or as your creative journey evolves.

Why it matters:

- *Emotional connection:* Music has the power to evoke strong emotions and can serve as a bridge between your passions and your creative work.

- *Inspiration:* A well-curated passion playlist can be a consistent source of inspiration, helping you get into the right mindset for your creative endeavors.

- *Mood enhancement:* Music can enhance your mood, boost motivation, and reduce stress, all of which contribute to a more productive creative process.

- *Personalization:* Creating your own passion playlist allows you to personalize your creative environment and infuse it with the energy of your passions.

- *Consistency:* Listening to your playlist regularly can help establish a consistent and focused creative routine. A passion playlist is a unique and personalized tool that can significantly impact your creative process. It connects your artistic passions with the emotional power of music, enhancing your creative mindset and fueling your artistic endeavors.

10. Passion portrait

What is it? A passion portrait is a visual representation of your creative passions and aspirations. It's a creative project that allows you to visually communicate the essence of what drives you and what you're passionate about in your creative journey.

How to do it:

1. ***Gather art supplies:*** Collect art supplies that resonate with you and your creative process. This might include drawing materials, paint, collage materials, or digital tools if you prefer a digital approach.

2. ***Set an intention:*** Before you begin, set an intention for your passion portrait. What message or emotions do you want to convey through your artwork? What aspects of your creative passions do you want to highlight?

3. ***Visual elements:*** Start by selecting visual elements that represent your passions. These could include symbols, colors, images, or abstract forms. Consider how each element contributes to the overall narrative of your portrait.

4. ***Layout and composition:*** Plan the layout and composition of your passion portrait. Decide how you'll arrange the chosen elements on your canvas or digital workspace. Experiment with different compositions until you find one that resonates.

5. ***Creation process:*** Begin creating your passion portrait. Whether you're drawing, painting, or digitally designing, let your intuition and emotions guide your creative choices.

6. ***Embrace imperfections:*** Don't be afraid to embrace imperfections or unexpected outcomes in your artwork. These can often add depth and authenticity to your passion portrait.

7. ***Incorporate text:*** Consider including words or phrases that hold personal significance related to your creative journey. These could be quotes, affirmations, or your own reflections.

8. *Express emotions:* As you work on your passion portrait, allow yourself to express the emotions and energy associated with your creative passions. Let your feelings flow into your artwork.

9. *Reflect and adjust:* Take breaks to step back and reflect on your progress. Assess how well your passion portrait aligns with your intention and make adjustments as needed.

10. *Final touches:* Once you're satisfied with your passion portrait, add any final touches or details that enhance the overall impact of your artwork.

11. *Share your portrait:* Share your passion portrait with your creative community or keep it as a personal symbol of your artistic journey.

Why it matters:

- *Visual representation:* A passion portrait visually represents the driving forces behind your creative journey, making them tangible and accessible.

- *Self-expression:* Creating art allows you to express complex emotions, experiences, and aspirations that might be challenging to convey through words alone.

- *Personal empowerment:* The process of creating a passion portrait can be empowering as it reinforces your connection to your creative passions and personal narrative.

- *Inspiration:* Your passion portrait can serve as a source of ongoing inspiration, reminding you of your artistic purpose and goals.

- *Storytelling:* It tells a visual story of your creative journey, capturing the essence of what motivates and inspires you. Creating a passion portrait is a deeply personal and artistic endeavor that can bring greater clarity and connection to your creative journey. It's a visual celebration of your passions and a testament to the power of artistic self-expression.

In the crucible of passion, we find the elixir of creativity. It is the divine fire that fuels our artistic journeys, the compass that guides us through adversity, and the bridge between our inner selves and the world. As we journey through this chapter, may you rekindle your own flame of passion and discover the profound transformations it can bring to your creative endeavors. In the words of Johann Wolfgang von Goethe, "Whatever you can do or dream you can do, begin it. Boldness has genius, power and magic in it. Begin it now." With the fire of passion burning brightly, we embark on the next chapter of our creative odyssey, ready to explore "The Wisdom of Patience."

9

The Power of Patience

In the world of professional boxing, the George Foreman versus Michael Moorer fight stands out as a prime example of the incredible power of patience. George Foreman, a boxing legend in his own right, had made a comeback to the sport after a ten-year hiatus. However, his return to the ring wasn't without its share of challenges.

Foreman had experienced a humiliating defeat in the past—an unforgettable loss to Muhammad Ali in Zaire. Foreman's patience, or lack thereof, was on full display in that infamous fight against Ali. He had entered the ring brimming with youthful exuberance, eager to knock out his opponent quickly. Yet Ali's tactical brilliance, coupled with Foreman's impatience, led to an embarrassing defeat. It was a pivotal moment in Foreman's career, one that he would never forget.

But it was precisely this defeat that would teach George Foreman the true value of patience. He realized that in the world of boxing, rushing to victory wasn't always the path to success. He understood that patience, in the form of calculated strategy and composure, could be his greatest ally.

George was a seasoned fighter at the age of forty-five, facing off against the much younger and reigning heavyweight champion, Michael Moorer. The match was a testament to Foreman's unwavering patience and his belief that time was on his side. For most of the fight, Moorer dominated, outpacing the aging Foreman with his speed and agility.

It seemed like the young champion had an insurmountable advantage. But Foreman had a plan, and he understood that patience could be his greatest ally. He knew that rushing to knock out Moorer wouldn't work; he had to wait for the right moment. Round after round, Foreman absorbed punches and kept his composure, all the while patiently waiting for an opening.

It was in the tenth round that Foreman's patience bore fruit. With a sudden burst of power and precision, he landed a devastating right hand that sent Moorer to the canvas. The count began, and by the time it reached ten, George Foreman had achieved the unthinkable. He became the oldest heavyweight champion in history, defying age and critics alike. This historic fight teaches us that, in the face of seemingly insurmountable odds, patience can be a game changer. Foreman's ability to endure, maintain composure, and strike at the right moment demonstrated the true essence of patience.

It's not just about waiting; it's about waiting for the right opportunity to make your move.

Patience in your creative journey

In my own life, I've experienced the contrasting outcomes of patience and impatience. There have been moments where impulsive decisions and a lack of patience led to setbacks and difficulties. I've rushed into projects or decisions, fueled by the desire for immediate results, only to find myself dealing with unintended consequences.

Conversely, when I've exercised patience, I've witnessed the beauty of thoughtful, well-planned achievements. My creative pursuits have been marked by moments when I meticulously plotted my course, taking one step at a time, fully aware that the journey might be long but worth every moment.

These moments of patience have led to some of my most significant artistic accomplishments. In my acting, writing, and even in the creation of my podcast, *Tales That Tickle*, original storytelling with first person characters, patience has been my guiding star. It has allowed me to craft stories with depth, characters with authenticity, and projects with lasting impact. Patience isn't just a virtue; it's a superpower that can transform creative ambitions into reality.

Exercise: *The Patience Inventory:* As you embark on your own creative journey, it's crucial to recognize the role of patience. To help you do this, I invite you to embark on a reflective exercise I like to call The Patience Inventory. Here's how it works:

1. Take out a piece of paper or open a digital document.

2. Divide the page into two columns. Label the left column "Moments of Patience" and the right column "Moments of Impatience."

3. Begin by jotting down instances in your life when patience has played a positive role. These could be personal achievements, creative breakthroughs, or moments of personal growth. Write a few sentences about each.

4. Next list situations where impatience may have led to challenges or difficulties. These might include instances where you rushed decisions, ignored important details, or sought shortcuts.

5. Reflect on the outcomes in both columns. Notice how patience has contributed to positive results and how impatience may have hindered progress.

6. Identify specific areas in your creative pursuits where you could benefit from practicing more patience.

7. Set concrete goals for cultivating patience in these areas. What steps can you take to be more patient in your creative process?

8. Keep this inventory as a reference and revisit it periodically to track your progress and celebrate your achievements. By

taking this inventory, you'll gain valuable insights into the role of patience in your creative journey. It's a step toward harnessing the superpower of patience and applying it purposefully in your pursuit of creative greatness.

George Washington Carver: A patient pioneer in agriculture

George Washington Carver was a renowned African American scientist and inventor who made remarkable contributions to agricultural science in the late nineteenth and early twentieth centuries. Born into slavery, Carver displayed an unwavering commitment to education and patience throughout his life. Carver's pioneering work in agricultural research, particularly in crop rotation and soil conservation, showcased his exceptional patience and dedication. He conducted countless experiments and patiently observed the growth of various crops. His research ultimately transformed farming practices in the American South, helping alleviate the region's dependence on cotton and improve soil quality. Despite facing significant racial discrimination and obstacles throughout his career, Carver remained patient and focused on his mission to improve the lives of farmers. His legacy serves as a testament to the transformative power of patience in achieving lasting change. In my own creative journey, I've often looked to figures like George Washington Carver for inspiration. Carver's patience in the face of adversity, his ability to persevere through setbacks, and his dedication to his craft all serve as reminders of the profound impact patience can have on one's creative endeavors.

Louis Pasteur: The patient pursuer of microscopic truth

Louis Pasteur, a French chemist and microbiologist in the nineteenth century, is celebrated for his groundbreaking work in the fields of microbiology and vaccination. His discoveries, such as the process of pasteurization and the development of vaccines for rabies and anthrax, have had an enduring impact on public health.

What sets Pasteur apart is his unwavering patience in unraveling the mysteries of the microscopic world. His meticulous and methodical approach to scientific inquiry involved countless experiments, observations, and recordkeeping over many years. Pasteur spent extensive periods observing microorganisms under his microscope, patiently documenting their behaviors and interactions.

One of Pasteur's most famous experiments involved disproving the theory of spontaneous generation, which suggested that life could arise spontaneously from nonliving matter. Through a series of carefully designed experiments, Pasteur demonstrated that microorganisms did not spontaneously generate but were introduced from external sources.

This groundbreaking work laid the foundation for our modern understanding of microbiology and disease transmission. Despite facing skepticism and opposition from some of his contemporaries, Pasteur's patience, commitment to scientific rigor, and meticulous documentation ultimately prevailed.

His discoveries revolutionized medicine and paved the way for the development of lifesaving vaccines. As we consider the life and work of Louis Pasteur, we can draw parallels between his patient pursuit of scientific truth and the patience required in our own creative journeys.

Pasteur's dedication to methodical experimentation and his refusal to rush his findings serve as a profound example of how patience can lead to transformative breakthroughs.

Exercise: The Patience Inventory: Reflect on the story of Louis Pasteur and the patience he exhibited in his scientific pursuits. Consider how his unwavering commitment to his work paid off in the form of groundbreaking discoveries. Then apply these insights to your own creative endeavors. Ask yourself: Where in your creative journey can you afford to be more patient? Are there areas where you've been rushing or seeking quick solutions? How might a more patient and methodical approach benefit your creative process? By learning from the patience of Louis Pasteur, you can embrace a deliberate and thoughtful approach to your creative work, allowing you to uncover new insights, overcome challenges, and achieve enduring impact.

Exercise 2: The Patience Inventory: As you embark on your creative journey, consider the stories of George Foreman, Muhammad Ali, and George Washington Carver. Reflect on their experiences and the role patience played in their successes. How can you apply the lessons of patience from these historical figures to your own creative pursuits? Use The Patience Inventory to identify areas where patience can be a superpower in your journey.

1. *Reflect on a recent situation where you felt impatient. What triggered your impatience, and how did it manifest in your thoughts and actions?*

2. *Think about a creative project or endeavor that required a significant amount of patience to complete. Describe the project and the challenges you faced in maintaining patience throughout its duration. How do you typically react when faced with unexpected delays or obstacles in your creative work?*

3. *Are there specific strategies or practices you employ to stay patient? Consider a historical figure known for their patience and perseverance.*

4. *What can you learn from their example in terms of maintaining patience in your own creative journey?*

5. *Have you ever abandoned a creative project prematurely due to impatience or frustration? Reflect on what led to that decision and whether there might have been a more patient approach.*

6. *Are there specific mindfulness or relaxation techniques you use to cultivate patience, especially during moments of creative frustration or stagnation?*

7. *Think about a time when patience paid off in a significant way in your creative work. How did your patience contribute to the success or satisfaction of that project?*

8. *Patience is often linked to resilience. Describe a situation in which your patience helped you bounce back from a setback or failure in your creative pursuits.*

9. *Consider how your understanding of the creative process has evolved in terms of patience.*

10. *Have you become more patient over time, and if so, what lessons or experiences contributed to this growth?*

11. *After completing the Patience Inventory, what insights or realizations have you gained about the role of patience in your creative journey?*

12. *How might you apply these insights moving forward?*

Rosa Parks: The quiet patience of a civil rights icon

Rosa Parks, often hailed as the "Mother of the Civil Rights Movement," displayed remarkable patience and unwavering resolve in the face of racial injustice in the mid-twentieth century United States. Parks' story is etched in history for her refusal to give up her seat on a segregated bus in Montgomery, Alabama, in 1955. While her act of civil disobedience is widely celebrated, what is less known is the patience and courage it took to reach that pivotal moment. Parks had long been an activist, working quietly but diligently for equality and civil rights. Her patience was evident in her dedication to the cause, even when progress was slow and obstacles were numerous. She served as the secretary of the Montgomery chapter of the NAACP and had been involved in numerous efforts to challenge segregation. When Parks made her historic stand by remaining seated, she didn't act on impulse. She had a wellspring of patience that allowed her to withstand the pressure and threats that followed. Her peaceful resistance sparked the Montgomery Bus Boycott, a seminal moment in the Civil Rights Movement.

Rosa Parks' legacy is a testament to the enduring power of patience and perseverance in the pursuit of justice and equality. Rosa Parks' story serves as a powerful reminder that patience is not limited to creative pursuits alone. It can also be a driving force behind social change and activism. The quiet yet unyielding patience displayed by Parks in the face of adversity can inspire us in our creative journeys. As we reflect on her life, let's consider how the lessons of patience, resilience, and unwavering commitment can be applied to our own creative endeavors. Parks' story illustrates that patience is not passive; it's an active force that can lead to transformative moments and lasting impact. Rosa Parks' story reminds us that patience isn't just about waiting; it's about standing firm in the face of adversity, refusing to be rushed, and persisting in the pursuit of what is right. In the world of creativity and beyond, patience can be a powerful ally, helping us overcome challenges, navigate obstacles, and ultimately make a meaningful difference. Her words resonate as a timeless reminder:

"I have learned over the years that when one's mind is made up, this diminishes fear; knowing what must be done does away with fear."

Sir Isaac Newton: Patience in pursuit of universal laws

Sir Isaac Newton, the brilliant English mathematician, physicist, and astronomer of the seventeenth century, is renowned for his foundational contributions to science. His laws of motion, law of universal gravitation, and development of calculus have had a profound and enduring impact on our understanding of the physical world. What might be less known is the extraordinary patience that underpinned Newton's groundbreaking discoveries. His work was characterized by painstaking attention to detail, relentless curiosity, and an unwavering commitment to unraveling the mysteries of the universe. One of Newton's most famous accomplishments was his formulation of the law of universal gravitation, which explained the force of attraction between all objects with mass. This discovery revolutionized our understanding of celestial bodies and their movements. However, it was the culmination of years of meticulous observations, mathematical calculations, and patient reflection. Newton's patience extended beyond his scientific pursuits. He famously remarked, "If I have seen further, it is by standing on the shoulders of giants," acknowledging the contributions of those who came before him. His humility and recognition of the patience of those who laid the groundwork for his discoveries exemplify the interconnectedness of patience and progress.

In our creative journeys, we can draw inspiration from Sir Isaac Newton's patient and methodical approach to discovery. Newton's work illustrates that patience is not merely the ability to wait but the capacity to persevere in the face of complex challenges and to persistently seek answers. Sir Isaac Newton's life and achievements remind us that patience is a potent force in the pursuit of knowledge, understanding, and creative breakthroughs. Whether we're exploring the laws of the universe or delving into the realms of art, music, or literature, Newton's example encourages us to embrace the patient pursuit of excellence and innovation.

By learning from the patience exhibited by these legendary individuals, you'll be better equipped to navigate the challenges and triumphs of your creative path. Remember that patience isn't just about waiting; it's about perseverance, thoughtful planning, and unwavering commitment to your creative goals.

Closing thoughts and quotes

In closing, the George Foreman versus Michael Moorer fight serves as a powerful reminder that patience, when wielded strategically, can lead to triumph in the most challenging circumstances. It's not about waiting idly; it's about waiting for the right moment to strike. As you reflect on your own journey, remember that the wisdom of patience can be your guiding light. Embrace it as a superpower that enables you to make well-considered decisions, weather creative storms, and ultimately achieve your artistic goals. Here are some quotes to inspire you on your path of patience:

> *Patience is not the ability to wait but the ability to keep a good attitude while waiting. (Joyce Meyer)*

> *Rivers know this: There is no hurry. We shall get there someday. (A. A. Milne, Winnie the Pooh)*

> *Patience and perseverance have a magical effect before which difficulties disappear and obstacles vanish. (John Quincy Adams)*

10

The Infinite Potential

In our journey through the realms of creativity, we've unveiled remarkable God superpowers—vision, resilience, inspiration, transformation, collaboration, empathy, focus, passion, and patience. As we ascend toward the apex of creative exploration, we reach the summit: *the infinite potential* that resides within each of us.

This chapter is a celebration of this ultimate superpower, one that transcends boundaries and propels us into the boundless realm of creativity. It's the realization that creativity is a divine gift, and words themselves hold immense power. Infinite potential isn't just an abstract concept; it's a profound truth. It's the understanding that the superpowers we've explored—vision, resilience, inspiration, transformation, collaboration, empathy, focus, passion, and patience—when combined, open the gateway to a world without limits. It's the recognition that creativity is not confined by definitions; it's an endless source that flows through every one of us.

Your journey has been filled with moments where you've tapped into this boundless source of creativity. Embrace those moments; they are your birthright. Each of the God superpowers you've encountered—vision, resilience, inspiration, transformation, collaboration, empathy, focus, passion, and patience—has been a transformative force in your creative journey. These powers, when combined with the superpower of creativity, create a synergy that propels you beyond ordinary creativity into the extraordinary.

163

The power you've discovered within yourself is not unique to your story. It's a universal truth that extends to all who dare to dream, create, and envision a better world. In this section, we extend an invitation to you, the reader, to embark on your journey of self-discovery and creative exploration. Practical exercises and thoughtful prompts await, encouraging you to identify your passions, nurture your vision, and practice patience on your path to unleashing your infinite potential.

Imagine a future where creativity knows no bounds, where technology amplifies your creative capabilities, and where your artistic contributions shape the world. The possibilities are limitless, and the future is yours to shape. We explore the role of AI and generative technology in expanding creative horizons and enabling new forms of artistic expression. Embrace this vision of a world where your infinite potential becomes a catalyst for transformation.

Growing up in a Christian family, the idea of using a title that could offend was a challenge. However, it illustrates the power of words and the idea that God is beyond definition. We dive into stories that showcase the profound impact of words and narratives on human history and creativity. In our closing moments, we invite you to engage in a final exercise.

Reflect on the journey you've taken through this book and create a personal declaration of your own infinite potential. Write it with the knowledge that words have the power to shape your reality. By acknowledging your own creative divinity, you amplify your infinite potential… As we conclude our journey, remember that the creative path is not a destination but a lifelong adventure. You are the author of your narrative, the artist of your canvas, and the creator of your world. The superpowers you've discovered within yourself are yours to wield, shaping your destiny and leaving an indelible mark on the tapestry of existence.

Closing thoughts and quotes

Follow on twitter @How2envy
@PhillipMitchellPolite on FB

I leave you with these powerful words:

Creativity is the greatest rebellion in existence. (Osho)

The most beautiful experience we can have is the mysterious—the fundamental emotion that stands at the cradle of true art and true science. (Albert Einstein)

The artist is a receptacle for emotions that come from all over the place: from the sky, from the earth, from a scrap of paper, from a passing shape, from a spider's web. (Pablo Picasso)

May you continue to embrace your infinite potential, wielding the superpower of creativity, and may your creativity be a force that defies boundaries, challenges norms, and transforms the world. Your journey has just begun.

About the Author

Brooklyn born and hailing from Jacksonville, Florida, he is a seasoned storyteller with a background in the military and the entertainment industry. A graduate of the New York Film Academy, he's been crafting stories since he was a child. Through *GodMode*, he invites readers on a transformative journey of self-discovery and creativity, drawing from his diverse life experiences and creative passions.

Milton Keynes UK
Ingram Content Group UK Ltd.
UKHW041308210924
1774UKWH00020B/39

9 798891 574397